WHEN A PAIR OF TOP-FLIGHT
REPORTERS MAKE THE SPORTS
WORLD THEIR BEAT—A BOOK
LIKE THIS IS BOUND TO HAPPEN

This book is based on the most extraordinary
newspaper sports column ever written—"Sports
Hot Line"—a column dedicated to unearthing
and reporting the answers to the most
challenging and irreverent questions fans
could conjure up.

You will discover how wild the questions could
be—and how frank the answers—in the
sophisticated and savvy sports book that holds
no one sacred, and holds nothing back
in telling you—

Everything You Always Wanted
to Know About Sports*

---

*and didn't know where to ask

EVERYTHING YOU ALWAYS WANTED TO KNOW ABOUT SPORTS*

*and didn't know
where to ask

by
Mickey Herskowitz
and
Steve Perkins

A SIGNET BOOK

SIGNET
Published by the Penguin Group
Penguin Books USA Inc., 375 Hudson Street,
New York, New York 10014, U.S.A.
Penguin Books Ltd, 27 Wrights Lane,
London W8 5TZ, England
Penguin Books Australia Ltd, Ringwood,
Victoria, Australia
Penguin Books Canada Ltd, 2801 John Street,
Markham, Ontario, Canada L3R 1B4
Penguin Books (N.Z.) Ltd, 182–190 Wairau Road,
Auckland 10, New Zealand

Penguin Books Ltd, Registered Offices:
Harmondsworth, Middlesex, England

First Signet Printing, June, 1977
17 16 15 14 13 12 11 10 9

REGISTERED TRADEMARK—MARCA REGISTRADA

Printed in the United States of America

Contents

FALL

WINTER

SPRING

SUMMER

Introduction

For generations, the American sports page had been a kind of scoreboard—describing who won, who lost, how they played the game. The belief was widely held that devout fans did not want to know if their favorite third baseman cheated on his wife, or that a wide receiver passed bad checks, or which basketball player packed a gun.

Then two things happened that changed the way the public thought about sports. Television chased the writers out of the press box in search of news the cameras couldn't show. And sports went to court. The secrets began to spill out. We read about player salaries so large they made your hair hurt.

And a new candor swept the land. No longer would fans be satisfied to know their hero's yards per carry or batting average. They demanded to know what he felt, his private pains and joys, what made him (and her) tick.

Blasphemy. But there it was. Sports had joined the real world. Frank Merriwell doesn't live here any more.

Some scholars point to one whimsical moment as the watershed of the revolution. After telephoning his wife, who had recently given birth, a winning pitcher returned to his locker, where a gaggle of reporters waited. "She was feeding the baby," he said proudly.

"Breast or bottle?" asked a reporter.

Such irreverent questions became the trademark of a new generation of sports reporters known as the chipmunks. Candor and wit and gossip were the fish they peddled.

Still, most newspapers were reluctant to allow a more "personal" journalism to appear in their regular news columns. Gambling, sex, and back-office scheming are subjects guaranteed to entertain readers. But they also tend to make publishers nervous. So the best answer was to create a new corner, a separate and different kind of sports feature. The concept was developed by John McMeel and Jim Andrews, who had founded the Universal Press Syndicate. They asked a Texas writing team, Mickey Herskowitz and Steve Perkins, to draw on their experience and contacts to produce "Sports Hot Line."

The philosophy was this: the people in sports, no matter how they isolate themselves and defy time and change, reflect the outside world; and they reflect it in a way that makes writing about them fun, for they do everything—well, nearly everything—before your eyes. It was inevitable that the public would want to know more about them than the information provided on the back of their bubble-gum cards. And if the athletes want to know what kept the kettle boiling, they need only to look in their own mirrors. An epidemic of sports books, under the let-it-all-hang-out banner, carrying such bylines as Jim Bouton and Joe Namath and Wilt Chamberlain, did more than anything to swing open locker-room doors.

In a sense, *Everything You Always Wanted to Know About Sports* is a dialogue with the new American fan, the best and most insightful questions collected over a four-year period. They are divided into seasons—seasons of sport, not of the calendar—and preceded by an interview with an athlete who captures the mood and quality of his game, of his time.

Many of the answers published here could not have appeared in print ten, or even five, years ago. Answers, hell. Until "Sports Hot Line" gave them space, not even such questions had appeared with any frequency in our daily sports pages. Now they are read in seventy-four newspapers with a combined circulation of over ten million subscribers.

Is this a good and healthy sign? Only if you enjoy the drama and nonsense behind the scoreboard, and if you look at athletes not just as jocks but as complete and interesting people.

—THE AUTHORS

FALL

How do you pick one player to capture the mystique of pro football, the new national religion? Do you go for the brute power of Nagurski, the leadership of Layne, the cool of Jim Brown? Or do you weigh Namath's headlines or Simpson's yards? Yet if you're looking for a storybook character, a man with the golden arm, there was only one. The six-dollar-a-game man, the ex-semipro quarterback who ushered the sport into its boom years.

Johnny Unitas:
The Football Player

Johnny Unitas left pro football pretty much as he came into it—without ceremony. One day he was still on the field, straining to recapture the rich talents of a spent career, and the next day he was sitting in front of a press conference, explaining dryly, "Your mind is willing but your body just wears out."

The scene was somewhat disjointed. Pickets milled outside the front gate. And the field—the one Unitas had walked away from—was on the wrong coast. It was catching a breeze off the blue Pacific, not Chesapeake Bay. For most of his fans, the time to get sentimental had been a year and a few months before, when the Baltimore Colts decided the services of Johnny U. were no longer needed. The treatment was cold and a little mean, but no worse, when you get right down to it, than England selling the London Bridge.

So Unitas, voted the greatest quarterback of pro football's first fifty years, ran out the string in San Diego, where the owner, Eugene Klein, called him "a living work of art." The dramatic gesture had always been alien to John's character, and to his style. Everything about him—his dress, his speech—suggested understatement, and this was the way he went out. He was on the practice field when the moment came. "The legs just wouldn't respond," he said. "They were sore and swollen and I couldn't maneuver. I stepped in a hole and sprained the left knee and the ankle, slightly. I was getting a message."

As he limped off the field, Unitas said to himself,

"It's time to get out." It was a Sunday morning and he went directly to Tommy Prothro, who had not exactly inherited a warm bed when he hired on to coach the Chargers.

"Tommy," said Unitas, in his best dropback-and-fire manner, "I think I'm gonna retire. I just can't do the things I'd like to do out there."

Prothro looked at him sympathetically. "That might be best, John," he said. "Must be embarrassing to someone like yourself, who has been able to do the things you've done, to find that it has become an effort."

"No," Unitas corrected him. "It's not embarrassing. It's just the fact that I can't do them."

And so it was done. No theatrics. No evasions. No cute exit lines. Just Johnny Unitas, speaking with a directness that erased all doubt, the way a wet thumb wipes chalk from a blackboard. It was one of the qualities we came to know and enjoy. Even when he sparred with the press—which he did well, if not always gladly—he was never subtle. He didn't exactly *trust* the press, see, but he wasn't paranoid about it. A moment flashes to mind from Super Bowl Week, the Colts against the Dallas Cowboys. During a gang interview, he was asked about the system then favored by Tom Landry, in which Craig Morton received all the plays from the bench.

John allowed that he could never tolerate such an arrangement. "You might as well have a dummy back there," he said. Suddenly he sat bolt upright and his eyes narrowed. "Now, don't you guys go writing that I called Morton a dummy. I *know* you guys."

It took a while, but the guys got to know him, too. They learned that he would not let you dig much below the surface. But his answers, far from being bland, had bite. And in all that he said or did, his enormous pride showed through.

I wondered, in that moment of melancholy that most men would feel, if Unitas thought about what

8

his life would have been like if he had not made that contact with the Colts, back in 1956.

"They called me," he said, a slight chill in his voice.

The question was rephrased. "Of course, they called you. But the connection. What if you hadn't connected with them. With any team. What would you have done?"

"I don't know," he said. "I don't think about things like that. What might have happened did happen."

There are not many cornball stories like it anymore. Getting cut by the Steelers. A season of semi-pro ball for the Bloomfield Rams at six bucks a game and getting paid in cash in the basement of a dairy. Then the call from the Colts and, shazam, two championships before the 50s had run out. He could do what the great ones always did: race the clock and bring his team from behind.

But he was much more than that. He may have been pro football's Last Hero. We have plenty of superstars, of course. Television and big money make them easy to find. But there are not many heroes left, of the kind little kids can admire and copy and whose stories are the kind you can read with your breakfast cereal. And that is what is poignant about the leave-taking of Johnny U.

You would not put it quite that way to Unitas, of course, unless you were prepared to watch a grown man throw up. But one got the idea across and Johnny thought about it.

"That's what disturbs me about so much of what is written today," he said. "The derogatory things. I know, the newspaper people say, 'We've got to print it like it is.' But I'd hate for my kids to idolize someone who is into drugs, who treats others with contempt, who thinks his talent is a license to behave any way he wishes. I've busted my ass all my life to watch where I go, what I do, with whom I'm seen. I spent nineteen years in it and a few guys make headlines for smoking pot and now the public thinks all pro football players are potheads.

"Some of the fun has gone out of the game. The thing that was so irritating was that the players coming into the league today wouldn't take the time, or put forth the effort, of those of ten and twelve years back. They were more concerned then with the game and the team. Little else mattered. You don't have that now. They don't want to spend the time.

"That's one reason I wouldn't want to coach. I couldn't put up with a lot of the horse manure the coaches take now from some of the players. I wouldn't have the patience with the phoniness of some of 'em, and the lack of dedication. I'd probably end up with a squad of twenty-five. There are too many factions on the teams now. You got everything from temperance guys to women's lib. It's like one fellow said: he had been with a team a year and he got traded before he could learn all the handshakes."

It was very much in character that Unitas would have been the first veteran to cross the picket line of the NFL Players Association, when the Chargers opened camp—his last camp—in the summer of 1974. "Football has given me every opportunity I ever had," he said simply. "No one else I know, from a poor section of Pittsburgh, from a poor family, has been able to sit down for lunch with three or four Presidents of the United States."

There is no record of anyone calling Johnny Unitas a scab.

In the end, Unitas had played out his uniform number—nineteen years. He was a winner. He was great. He brought us to the stadium and he made us cheer. He attempted more passes and completed more, for more yards and touchdowns, than anyone else who had ever played the game.

Of course, it was a job and he was well paid for it, and maybe there is no need to romanticize what he did. But there is a suspicion that we will not see another like him. The urge was to not let him get away unapplauded. "I came into the league without any fuss," he said. "I'd just as soon have left it that way. There's no difference that I can see in retiring from pro football or quitting a job at the Pennsy Railroad. I did something I wanted to do, and went as far as I could go."

To appreciate how far, you have to know the conditions under which he came to the Baltimore Colts. Weeb Ewbank was looking for a backup quarterback (to Gary Shaw) when he invited Unitas to a tryout camp. "He came in," recalled Weeb, "and we took pictures of him in practice. Not movies. *Still* pictures. In those days, we didn't have any film equipment. The only good the stills did was when you had a bunch of kids at a tryout, you could keep the pictures in front of you and it helped to remember which ones they were.

"We took pictures of John under center, and again when he set up and right at the last, when he followed through. That was the thing we noticed right away, how he followed through. It was exceptional. The pictures showed it clearly. His arm went through so far that he turned his hand over like a pitcher. I often wondered how he kept from injuring his arm, because it was like throwing a screwball, and all those guys ended up with crooked arms. When he followed through, his fingers turned over and you could see the back of his hand. And when he used to throw a lot of times, with his tremendous follow-through, he'd snag his fingernails on the back of a guy's shirt or he'd jam his fingers on somebody's helmet. He had to be careful of that. I worried that he might get what they call a tennis elbow but, boy, I saw the way he could throw and I never bothered him about it. You knew right away. He was in camp no time at all and we knew that as soon as he learned the offense he would be our quarterback."

Years later Ewbank would be across the field, coaching Joe Namath and the New York Jets, on what may have been the saddest day of John's career—the day the Jets upset the Colts. Unitas spent most of the game as a spectator, coming off the bench late in the third quarter, trying to wake up the echoes one more time, rallying the Colts as he had done so often. And on the Jets' bench a strange thing happened. Seeing the quarterback he had developed at Baltimore, Ewbank forgot himself. Weeb actually clapped his hands and shouted out to the field, *"No interceptions now, John."*

Later, when it was over, a writer asked Unitas, "How good is Joe Namath?"

"Sixteen to seven," Unitas replied, saying it all.

Carroll Rosenbloom, who owned the Colts then (and now the Rams), and whose relationship with Unitas was almost paternal, got his first tip about the crewcut Louisville University product from Art Rooney, whose Steelers had rejected him. "He had been in camp a few days," recalled Rosenbloom, "and Rooney called me about something or other. He said, 'Carroll, you got that boy Uni-TASS. I want to tell you something. My sons tell me that guy was the best-looking quarterback we had in camp and my coach [Walt Kiesling] never let him THROW the ball.' After that, I watched John in practice. He was so relaxed, so loose, and a very likable kid. This whole time we were wondering if we needed to trade for another quarterback, or if Unitas could do the job backing up George Shaw. We went into Chicago and were leading that game by ten points and, in the middle of the second quarter, they ruined Shaw's career. The Bears hit him high and low and across the mouth, broke his nose and knocked out most of his teeth. He was a sight. They had to carry Shaw off, and Unitas had to come into the game. I must say he looked horrible and we lost it [58 to 27]; in fact, the first pass Unitas threw was intercepted for a touchdown.

"I went down to the locker room. John was never one to show his emotions, but he was sitting in front of his locker, still hadn't taken off his uniform and had his head hanging between his legs so that all you could see was the top of that crewcut. I walked over and got him under the chin and lifted his head up. I said, 'Now, look, John, that was not your fault. You haven't had an opportunity to play and no one is blaming you. You're not only going to be a good one in this league, you're going to be a *great* one.'

"Well, I was just trying to build him up, get him out of the dumps. I wasn't sure right then he'd even make the club. But many times over the years John would ask me about that, how I could be so sure he'd make it. I'd tell him, 'What the hell, John, I'm an old jock. I know talent.' "

Johnny Unitas knew he had arrived—knew he had it made—when he returned to New York two weeks after quarterbacking the Colts to that colossal victory over the Giants in the title game of 1958. The Colts had won in sudden death, in what was to become The Greatest Game Ever Told.

He and his wife wandered into what was then one of the city's most exclusive night spots, the Harwyn Club. The headwaiter recognized him—the hot new celebrity in town. "Right this way, Mr. Unitas," he sang out. They were led to a corner table, the most prominent in the joint. It was at *that* very table, the headwaiter confided proudly, that Eddie Fisher and Liz Taylor had their rendezvous the night before Eddie flew home to Hollywood to tell Debbie Reynolds he wanted a divorce.

It was not your ordinary table. It was not your ordinary decade, either. But Johnny Unitas was right for the times and perfect for pro football, which had begun to take off. The 1958 sudden-death encounter, more than any other single event, gave the game new visibility, and Johnny U. was its hero.

With a touch of irony, Unitas says, "I've always felt that it wasn't a real good football game until the last two minutes, and then the overtime. We played pretty well but we should have blown New York out of the stadium and we didn't. Then we had to come from behind in order to tie and then go on to win it. Just the fact that it was the first overtime in championship play, that was enough to make people feel they had seen something fantastic.

"They always forget that the month before, in the game that clinched the division championship and put us into the playoff, San Francisco had us down twenty-seven to seven at the half and we came back to beat 'em [35 to 27]. That was a much better game. Our defense shut out Y. A. Tittle in the second half, and that was quite an accomplishment."

You ask Unitas how it feels and what it has meant to him, those nineteen years, and what he thought when they were over, at a moment when most men would be up to their eyeballs in melancholy. It was like asking him to say something in a foreign language.

"I'm not philosophical," he reminded, "one way or another. With me it has always been point blank, yes, no, can you or can't you. I just couldn't play anymore. It was time to quit and get out. I was taking up someone else's time.

"The people you meet, the friendships, the characters you have the enjoyment of playing with—there have been so many: Alex Hawkins, Big Daddy Lipscomb, Jim Parker, Bert Rechichar. I could name a dozen—that's what you take out of it. For me the thrill wasn't only in winning. It was working with people who were as dedicated as you are, working at times like a big machine.

"Mentally, I haven't changed. I feel the same. I care the same. If I could have gotten a leg transplant I'd probably have played for another thirty years. But I couldn't move anymore. The way it was, it was like standing in the middle of a road and saying, 'Okay, Buick, run me down.' "

Maybe one only imagined it, but a little emotion, a glimpse of regret, seemed to flicker lightly between the words. You have to look closely, of course. For nineteen years Unitas had been about as emotional as a large rock. He had made a point of noting that the legs, not the golden arm, finally undid him. It was a touch of pride no one could begrudge him.

On the other hand he was hardly humorless. His was a wry kind of wit, the kind that worked for a slow grin, not a belly laugh. Once he said he never believed in looking back, and he added a familiar line, "Something might be gaining on you."

He was told that he had selected a quote from a profound source, and he seemed honestly unaware. "Who said it?" he asked. "Paul Brown? Benjamin Franklin?"

"One of your contemporaries," came the reply. "Satchel Paige."

"Oh," said Unitas. "Is he considered old?"

Another time he described what it was like in the huddle: "When the score's loose, and you're way ahead, even the guards are offering you plays. When it gets nice and tight, you ask somebody for help and you don't hear a damned thing."

Somehow, you can't imagine it having happened very often, Johnny U. asking for help.

Questions & Answers

Q: *With the possible exception of Bart Starr, wasn't Otto Graham the squarest, straightest NFL quarterback of modern times?—Alan D., Shaker Heights, Ohio.*

A: Otto didn't drink, didn't smoke, didn't chew, and didn't go with girls who do. His roommate on a Browns road trip was therefore relieved to find that the quarterback was human. "The first thing Otto did, when he checked into a hotel," remembers the roomie, "was drag out a pair of binoculars big enough for Yamamoto in the Battle of the Coral Sea. Then he beamed in on the hotel rooms across the block. I kind of liked the guy after I knew what his hangup was."

Q: *I've read about Jimmy The Greek getting head-to-head with oilman H. L. Hunt on college football. How did it end, or who busted out whom? —Si Goldberg, Miami.*

A: In the late 50s, Jimmy Snyder and the old man high-rolled it into six-figure bets on Southeastern and Southwest Conference football. The series ended with Hunt owing The Greek 65Gs. Hunt stopped all pay-offs when he was stiffed on a $2 million parlay by a Chicago syndicate.

Q: *Dave Meggessey said there were some non-heterosexual goings-on in NFL shower rooms. True or false? —Ernie Zofko, Gary.*

A: False. But—only a few years ago a number one draft choice was waived out of the league after one season because he was a homosexual.

Q: *Vince Lombardi is already a legend equal to Knute Rockne, and that's okay with me. But Vince's line, "Winning isn't everything . . . it's the only thing," wasn't original, was it? Didn't Bear Bryant say it first? —Charley W., Birmingham.*

A: Lombardi picked that up at West Point. On the eve of the Navy game in 1944, the Army team received a telegram that included the deathless phrase about winning. It was from the Phillippines, signed Douglas MacArthur.

Q: *I have an argument with some friends who say Johnny Unitas is the best pro quarterback ever. I come from way back and I say Sammy Baugh was the best, because he was a punter and played defense. Wasn't Baugh an outstanding defensive back, or did they just hide him back there because rules said he had to play both ways? —Will G., Washington, D. C.*

A: Baugh is in the NFL record book as a defensive back. He shares with ten others the mark for most interceptions in a game, four.

Q: *What I can't understand about Joe Namath is that he makes all those TV commercials, plus three movies, the cool Luke of pro football, and yet he came out of Beaver Falls and Tuscaloosa. That the University of Alabama put that polish on him I can't believe.* —*Joseph V., Philadelphia.*

A: For answer, we will give you artist LeRoy Neiman's impression of Joe Willie when he arrived in New York: "I first saw him at Dudes-'n-Dolls. He looked like he came out of where he came out of. He was wearing an I.D. bracelet, and he was dressed like a used-car salesman. He was drinking beer with a go-go dancer." The Big A., not Alabama, put the polish on him, man.

Q: *Pro basketball doesn't seem to care any more weather a kid has finished playing college ball before signing him as a "hardship case." How long has the NFL observed its rule about not signing collegians?* — *Charles V., Philadelphia.*

A: NFL old-timers such as Halas and Rooney refer to it as "The Pledge," which the league adopted in 1926. Revocation of The Pledge meant a fine of $1,000, or the loss of the franchise. In those days a fine of $1,000 would probably have meant loss of franchise.

Q: *I saw Miami owner Joe Robbie on national television after the 1974 Super Bowl. This guy didn't look like he could run a filling station. I understand he was nothing until he finagled an AFL franchise, but I don't know the details. How did he get where is is?* —*Elliott P., Carbondale, Illinois.*

A: Joe got where he is, specifically, by having the genius to give Don Shula 12 percent of the ball club. Robbie was a Minneapolis attorney, in the $25,000 bracket, when a Philly client asked him to intercede with Robbie's old South Dakota pal, Joe Foss, then president of the AFL. Foss didn't want an AFL team in Philly and preferred Miami. Foss suggested Robbie himself apply for the Miami site. "When you have the franchise," Foss explained, "you'll find the money." Robbie bought the Dolphins the way an ordinary guy would kite a check.

Q: *I think Craig Morton is a hunk of a doll. Is he married? Has he ever been married?* —Susan L., St. Louis.

A: Quarterback Morton married his college sweetheart during his senior year at the University of California, signed for a big bonus, then was divorced before he reported to the Dallas Cowboys, thus learning about the California community property laws. He has not wed since.

Q: *I was listening to a local disc jockey and he asked a way-out question which he was supposed to answer later. I missed the answer and it's driving me up the wall. There were two quarterbacks who played in Yankee Stadium with the same initials—Y.A.T. Naturally, everybody knows that one was Y. A. Tittle, but I can't believe anybody else had the same initials.* —Eddie D., Rochester, New York.

A: Sorry you had to ask. This took hours and hours of research and almost drove us up the wall. The answer is Young Arnold Tucker, Army quarterback in the great 0–0 battle with Notre Dame in 1946. Tittle's initials, by the way, stand for Yelberton Abraham.

Q: *Johnny Cash's hit, "A Boy Named Sue," was supposedly inspired by a famous sports figure, but I never heard or read about anybody that even had such a nickname. Have I got the wrong dope?* —Louis Markol, Chester, Pennsylvania.

A: Closest we can come to your answer is the daddy of football's Jim Brown, known as Swinton (Sweet Sue) Brown, gambling man, as his son identifies him. Says Brown: "Friends called him just plain Sue. He was a huge man who had been a good football player in Brunswick, Georgia. He boxed professionally around

18

the state. He loved to dance and fancied himself a man-about-town. It just happened that he had a weakness for dice and cards. Sue always figured that Lady Luck was due to smile on him, but she mostly turned her back."

Q: *Jack Pardee, the coach of the Washington Capitals in the World Football League, coached in college one year, didn't he? And isn't he the only guy who ever came back and played after being a college coach? —Don Cartwell, Pittsburgh.*

A: Not since the days of Centre College and the Praying Colonels has anyone done it. Pardee left the Rams to coach linebackers at Texas A&M in 1965, but returned when George Allen became head man at LA in 1966. There is more to this story—Pardee was the victim of one of the deadliest types of cancer, melanoma, which only one in four survives. The mole was on Pardee's upper inside right arm. It took Pardee that year on the sidelines to recover physically. He played six seasons after that, ending up in the Super Bowl with Washington against Miami.

Q: *In his playing prime who was the meanest, toughest, smartest, best linebacker, Ray Nitschke or Dick Butkus? —Dick Christiansen, Sacramento.*

A: All we can tell you is Dick Butkus was All-NFL with a loser, Nitschke was All-NFL with a winner. Interestingly, off the field both are gentle homebodies, though Nitschke was once a carouser. After he changed his ways, teammate Dan Currie asked him, "Hey, Ray, what's it like, not drinking?" Nitschke looked at him a moment and said, "It's quiet, man. Real quiet."

Q: *Who was the original Fearsome Foursome in football, the Vikings, or the Rams, or somebody else? —Homer Nagel, Lima, Ohio.*

A: The term is a longtime football cliché, once used in referring to various college backfields. But in pro terms, the "real original" Fearsome Foursome tag fits

the Los Angeles defensive line of the early 1960s—
tackles Merlin Olsen and Roosevelt Grier, ends Lamar
Lundy and Deacon Jones, as immortalized in the
famous quatrain: "Olsen, Rosey, Lundy, and Jones; a
Fearsome Foursome to rattle your bones. When the
quarterback asks which were the ones, tell him Olsen,
Rosey, Lundy, and Jones."

Q: *The pro football players call the owners pinch-
penny and yet it seems to me the players are the real
cheapskates for not including old-timers who kept the
game going so many years for almost no money. If the
old guys were let into the pension plan, would it wreck
the program? How much of a problem is this?* —*Cary
Noughton, San Antonio.*

A: According to the NFL Alumni Association, the
old-timers (retired prior to 1959) group led by Leon
Hart, there are only 411 living exes who would qualify.
What particularly galls the vets is that the first player
due to get a pension check is a field goal specialist,
Ben Agajanian. Ben was a specialist, but not by design.
He lost the toes of his right foot in an elevator accident
as a college boy. His pro career spanned eighteen
years, with nine teams, in three leagues. A kicking
candidate once looked at Ben's foot and asked, "How
can I get a shoe to fit like yours?" Ben said, "First, you
get a hatchet . . ."

Q: *Who has the most football yards in one season
as a quarterback?* —*Jim Hawkins, Chicago.*

A: Joe Namath of the New York Jets, in that wonderful year 1967. He passed for 4,007 yards in the
regular season. Second and third places are both held
by Sonny Jurgensen of Washington (1967) and Philadelphia (1961), some 300 yards behind Joe.

Q: *Until the World Football League came into the
news, I thought the oddest name in sports was the
Browns. I realize the Cleveland coach's name was*

Brown, but otherwise what is a Brown? —*Ralph Bennings, Cincinnati.*

A: Owner Mickey McBride staged a contest for the fans to name the team in 1946. The winner, worth $1,500, was Panthers. But the owner of a semi-pro team in the area protested he already owned the Cleveland Panthers. McBride happily staged another contest, choosing "Brown Bombers" in honor of the popular heavyweight champ. The name was shortened to Browns, as McBride knew it would be.

Q: *What takes place in the defensive huddle? I have noticed that the spokesman for the defense glances over to the linesman to see how much yardage is needed by the opponent. Then, as his group goes into a huddle, what does he say?* —*Henry M. Gaines, San Pedro, California.*

A: The defensive signal caller, almost always the middle linebacker, may look at the yardmarker as you say, but he's more likely looking at the coach on the sidelines who actually calls the defense to be used. After getting this hand signal, he'll pass it on as follows: "Okay, let's play a 33 (pass coverage) and in the line let's play a flex strong. Watch the X end [tight end] on this one."

Q: *Sports pages are really great for giving you figures out of thin air. You said the NFL is about 40 percent black players and at the same time admitted nobody is counting. So how can you back up the percentage? Personally, I don't care what the percentage is as long as they select players on ability.* —*Vince D'Antoni, Seattle.*

A: It so happens that *Ebony* magazine is counting —they point out that last season 198 coaches coached 1,118 NFL players, of whom 435 are black, and yet only five of the coaches are black. That works out to about 39 percent plus some change. The high and low totals in the league include Chicago (25), San Diego

(22), Dallas (21), NY Giants (9), New Orleans (9), and Miami (12).

Q: *You said John Brodie got $910,000 during the bidding wars. I wonder how much income tax he paid on this amount? Also, when you hear of these fantastic amounts, does Uncle Sam always get his cut of the pie?* —*Erwin Hauser, St. Louis.*

A: You better believe it. The catch is that the high-bonus totals—a settlement in Brodie's case—are routinely postponed and spread out over a number of years to lessen the tax bite. Brodie will be collecting most of his money for the next ten years, as he begins his career as a network commentator.

Q: *It doesn't seem like fifteen years since the American Football League started up. Wasn't Billy Cannon the first player the AFL drafted? In fact, can you give me the AFL's first round and what happened to them?* —*George Regnary, Butte.*

A: Gerhard Schwedes, Syracuse running back, was the first pick (Boston), failed to make the team, wound up working in the office. The rest of the first round went in order: Richie Lucas, Don Meredith, Roger LeClerc, Billy Cannon, Monty Stickles, Dale Hackbart, and George Izo. Four of them signed with the NFL, and only Cannon made it in the new league.

Q: *I was in Vegas last week and saw half a dozen pro football players [names omitted] at the tables. Isn't this a pretty dicey situation for them to be in? Doesn't the league have a rule that covers this?* —*Cap Vickers, Seattle.*

A: Las Vegas is so clean it's a Disneyland for Adults. The NFL players, moreover, are aware of impressions and are constantly reminded they must remain above suspicion. While doing TV commercials in New York recently, Jimmy The Greek Snyder beat Roger Staubach out of one dollar in a quickie poker game between takes. When Staubach paid up, Snyder pushed the bill back to him and grinned. "Keep it," he said. "In a week it would be all over the country that Jimmy The Greek cleaned out Roger Staubach in a high stakes poker game."

Q: *A friend offered to bet me there are five methods of scoring in a football game, and I can count only four—TD, field goal, safety, and the extra point. Is this a trick question? He won't tell me the fifth unless I put up my money. —Ernie Gordon, Macon, Georgia.*

A: No trick. The fifth method is via "palpably unfair play." Greatest example of this occurred January 1, 1954, when Alabama's Tommy Lewis came off the bench to tackle Rice's Dicky Moegle when he was in the clear for a Cotton Bowl touchdown. Rice was awarded the touchdown.

Q: *I know that the Baltimore Colts got Johnny Unitas for a postage stamp or a seventy-five-cent phone call, but I have never read why they were digging that deep for a quarterback, or when they decided to keep him. —John C. Larned, Atlanta.*

A: In 1956 a Colt backup quarterback, Garry Kerkorian, retired to attend law school, and Coach Weeb Ewbank suddenly remembered a stoop-shouldered kid he had wanted to draft the year before when Pittsburgh had taken him. The phone call resurrected Unitas from the minor leagues.

Q: *I keep up with pro football, and I know the rule on punts is that only the two outside men can go downfield before the ball is kicked. My buddy argues that a third man can cross the line before it's kicked, but that's all he'll say except "look it up." Is he kidding me? —Danny Cerudo, Pittsburgh.*

A: Hoo, boy, can you lose the house and lot on this one! The third man who can cross the line before the ball is kicked is the punter—and then he can kick it!

23

NFL rules have always provided that the ball can be punted from anywhere on the field.

Q: *Somewhere in my travels, dreams, imagination, I came up with this statement: When Bronko Nagurski was presented with a ring (Hall of Fame, All-American, or whatever), the newsmen noted the fact that a standard size golf ball would roll through it. Did I dream, or is it true? —H. F. Gardner, South Gate, California.*

A: Nagurski's ring, presented to him at the Canton, Ohio, Pro Football Hall of Fame in 1967, is a size 19½. The jewelers, the famed Balfour Company, say it is the largest ring ever made in the U. S. It took them four years to construct it because they had no dies that size and new molds kept shattering. As for the golf ball, if Bronko wanted a golf ball to go through there, it would.

Q: *I have tried to read everything I can about our President, but I get different stories on the front page and the sports page about his football days. Can you set out the facts as to whether he was an All-American? —John Horvath, St. Louis.*

A: President Ford's athletic background is authentic and lustrous and needs no exaggeration. He was a substitute center on the great Michigan teams of 1932 and 1933 because the starter was an All-American. As a senior, teammates voted him MVP.

He was not All-American but did play in the East–West Shrine game and got an offer of $200 a game from Green Bay Packer coach Curley Lambeau. Ford turned this down and accepted a job as assistant coach at Yale, so that he could enter law school. He doubled as coach of the boxing team. He coached at Yale for six seasons, getting a peak salary of $3,600 and earning his law degree before entering World War II. Other assistants on that Yale staff were Greasy Neale, later to coach the Philadelphia Eagles to NFL titles, and

24

Ivy Williamson, who became an established head coach at Wisconsin.

Q: *Lyndon Johnson said President Ford played too much without a helmet, which doesn't sound so funny now. But did Ford ever actually play in a game without his helmet? Did players really do this in the 1930s? —C. J. Silvera, Sacramento.*

A: Ford never played without his helmet but did not wear one in posed pictures of him in uniform. Quite a few players in the early 30s thought it was manly—or less cumbersome—to play without a helmet. The last famous player we know of who did not wear headgear was the two-time All-America end from LSU, Gaynell (Gus) Tinsley in 1936.

Q: *A lot of politicians have gone out of their way to show they are sports-minded. I think Nixon ran this in the ground, too. The new President was a college football player, so is he going to lay on more of the same? The "how you play the game" line is wearing thin. —Charles Cotton, Portland, Oregon.*

A: There's an essential difference here. Richard Nixon was a genuine fan, with the fan's naïveté. If ever President Ford enters a locker room it will be with familiarity, because he has been there. He makes no apologies for his references to sports: "I know I am guilty of leaning heavily on football jargon, but for two reasons I think this is understandable. First, there is a great social significance to the game. The athletes are highly skilled, but subservient to the team. Yet if they do their jobs, they give an individual an opportunity for stardom. I know of no other sport that demands so much and returns so much. The second reason is that I truly enjoyed my football experience and just don't want to forget it."

Q: *I like to have a little something going when I watch pro football, and last season this got expensive.*

Do you know how the big boys bet their money? Do they have any tips on betting the pros? —Arnold Keaton, Philadelphia.

A: The high rollers spend more time on their bets than you spend on your job. But here's a shortcut: compare the opening line on Tuesday with the adjusted line on Saturday, then bet AGAINST the change. You will, in effect, be betting against the public, and the public is almost always wrong. Other tips: Bet the favorite, especially when spotting seven points or less. Over the past two seasons in the NFL, favorites beat the spread 198 times, while underdogs won 154. Never bet an underdog unless you think the team can win outright. You might also invest $1.75 in the Dell paperback, *The National Football Lottery,* by Larry Merchant, the most complete and entertaining book written about pro football betting. Merchant tells how he won $18,109 in the 1973 season.

Q: *I have been a pro football fan for several years but am embarrassed to admit that I do not know the full significance of the two-minute warning. Could you please explain? —B. F. Powell, Pasadena, Texas.*

A: Before the two-minute period was instituted at the close of each half, NFL teams used so many dodges to halt the clock (fake injuries, etc.) that the league had to formulate special rules for those dramatic intervals. The coaches are in effect being put on notice that the two-minute rules are taking over. One example is on a kickoff. During the rest of the game, the clock starts when the kicker boots the ball. In the two-minute period the clock doesn't roll until a member of the receiving team touches the ball. Another is that an injury timeout is charged during the two-minute time period. On other occasions it is an officials' time-out.

Q: *How many scholarships does Notre Dame give for its football program and how much do they spend on football? —K. J. Flanigan, East St. Louis.*

A: The Irish give the same number of scholarships as any other NCAA school—thirty a year, but as you might expect, they are highly selective. Father Edmund Joyce says about the profits: "Football covers the cost of our entire athletic program. That is, football profits support our fencing team and the rest. After all that, it nets us between $200,000 and $300,000 a year."

Q: *Could you please name some pro coaches who don't have playing experience?* —*Sparky Kleinschmidt, Houston.*

A: We assume you mean college experience. Head coaches who never played as pros outnumber the others by 16-10. Only one NFL head coach, Rick Forzano, never played football after age fourteen, when he was kneed in the eye in a high school game at Akron. Forzano has since suffered impaired vision, though he memorized the eye chart to enlist in the Marines at seventeen. He was studying physical education at Kent State under the late Don McCafferty when a nearby high school asked the department for an unpaid volunteer to coach its team. Forzano obliged, heading up on the ladder.

Q: *Whatever happened to the $18 million the Jets and Oakland were supposed to pay the Giants and the 49ers as a merger fee? Are they paying it?* —*Harry Klassen, King of Prussia, Pennsylvania.*

A: The nine ex-AFL teams pay it all right, just as regularly as the old home mortgage. Each club coughs up $100,000 annually. The payment, which Oakland's Al Davis still calls "total blackmail," is split $500,000 to the Giants and $400,000 to San Francisco. This goes on until 1987.

Q: *Has there ever been a teenage pro football player? If not, who was the youngest, and how old?* —*Tommy Fotch, Houston.*

A: Danny Fortmann, Colgate lineman, was nineteen when he reported to the Chicago Bears training camp the summer of 1936. Fortmann turned twenty before the season started. He is the youngest in NFL records. Also a great one. Fortmann is now a doctor in Burbank, California.

Q: *Baseball players have a lot of superstitions, like stepping on third base every inning going to their position. I was wondering if you know of any such superstitions in pro football? —Dick Finley, Norfolk, Virginia.*

A: Many coaches have erstwhile lucky coats or caps they wear on the sidelines. The most interesting superstition we know of was owner Carroll Rosenbloom's cigar act during Baltimore games, before he gave up smoking and gave up the Colts. Rosenbloom kept two cigars going simultaneously. He would puff on one when his team was on offense, then switch to the other for defense.

Q: *Has a pro football game ever been postponed because of weather? —Tommy Fotch, Houston.*

A: No, but there was a close call on the 1967 championship game at Green Bay (vs. Dallas) when the mercury dropped overnight to 12-below. Among things we never learned until now: league officials spent all night debating postponement before deciding at 6:00 A.M. to go on with the game. Bart Starr and Jerry Kramer were grateful, but six players and three officials got frostbite.

Q: *The NFL put in a whole lot of rules this year to change the game and make it high scoring, but in every game I see one team looks like another with the same stereotyped offense. Isn't it true nobody has tried anything different since years ago when the shotgun offense had a brief trial? —Frank Kelly, Philadelphia.*

A: You don't know what you've been seeing. This

has long been a bad rap against the NFL, where offenses on most teams combine elements of the single wing, split-T, double wing, the "I" and spread (slot) formations. There is far more variety in the pros than in the colleges, where they either go with the veer or the wishbone.

Q: *Do the San Diego Chargers still have a team psychiatrist? They seem to be playing better this year and I wondered if the shrink had anything to do with it?* —Cass Horton, Carbondale, Illinois.

A: Dr. Arnold Mandell, professor of psychiatry at UC-San Diego, was an inside observer of the Chargers in 1972 and 1973. He finally concluded that psychiatry and football don't mix, but he also came up with some insights on the psyches of different pro positions. The offensive linemen are conservatives who prefer structure and discipline. Defensive linemen are generally incorrigible challengers to rules of behavior. Wide receivers are vain and solitary people. Linebackers play for internal satisfaction more than any other pros. Defensive backs are more inclined to be suicidally depressed. So what else is new?

Q: *I am an old St. Mary's Gaels fan, which should date me fairly well. It saddens me to see the heroes of my era pass away with such little notice. I am thinking especially of Jimmy Phelan, who coached St. Mary's when they went to the Sugar Bowl and later coached in the pro leagues. I think he deserves more than a line at the bottom of the page.* —Cornelius Shanklin, San Mateo, California.

A: Phelan, who quarterbacked Notre Dame before World War I, indeed deserves to be remembered for the warmth of his personality, if not his won-lost records. While head man of the 1952 Dallas Texans (in the NFL), it was not rare for Phelan to call off the day's practice and take the entire team to the racetrack. Texan quarterback Bob Celeri, now an assistant at Buffalo, has a vivid memory of Phelan's coaching tactics: "I'd hit a couple of passes and it was the first time all day we had been in the other end of the field. Phelan motioned for a time-out and called me over to the sidelines. He had a cigar in one hand and he clapped me on the shoulder with the other. He said, 'Bobby, get us a touchdown.' I said okay and on the next play I threw a touchdown pass. While everybody was jumping up and down, it struck me what Phelan had done. Everybody in the ball park thought he had given me a TD play."

Q: *When did pro football players quit using the old leather helmets and go to the hard plastic jobs? And wasn't Elroy Hirsch the first to wear a plastic helmet?* —*Steve Melnyk, Columbus, Ohio.*

A: The plastic headgear began to appear right after the war, in 1945, when the supply of plastic was plentiful again. But various Chicago Bears and a few others around the league wore leather helmets into the 50s.

After Hirsch suffered a second, serious head injury, in 1949, the coach of the Rams, Clark Shaughnessy, had a special helmet designed from a light, extra strong plastic that had been used in the construction of fighter plane fuel tanks. The helmet weighed only eleven ounces, about one third of the weight of the leather models. It was soon widely copied.

Q: *Am I wrong, or wasn't Terry Bradshaw a surprise pick when the Steelers took him Number 1 in the draft in 1970? I recall people saying what a gamble it was, to take a quarterback who hadn't played against major college teams.* —*Arthur Gleason, Jr., Miami.*

A: Bradshaw's selection out of Louisiana Tech was no surprise to the pro scouts, who described him as the kind of prospect "who comes along once every ten or twelve years." The only question was whether the Steelers would trade his draft rights for established players. The Cardinals, among others, offered four starters. The venerable Art Rooney, for the only time in his Pittsburgh ownership, intervened in the draft, and insisted that the team keep Bradshaw. "I was tired," he said, "of giving away great players and suffering through fifteen years of them coming back to town with other teams." The list of quarterbacks let go by the Steelers includes Johnny Unitas, Len Dawson, Jack Kemp, Bill Nelsen, and Earl Morrall. Adds Rooney: "We even had the rights to Sid Luckman and lost those. I didn't want to see it happen again."

Q: *After reading about the antics of Coach Woody Hayes of Ohio State, I am curious about what kind of example such men must be setting for their players. What do the players say about him, or are they allowed to express an opinion? I am a retired high school teacher and football coach. —Gus Hudspeth, Colorado Springs.*

A: Pete Cusick, the Ohio State lineman who was one of the four finalists for the Vince Lombardi Award, in 1975, put it this way: "Coach Hayes is like anyone else. He shows his emotions. When he's angry, he shows it. And when he's happy he doesn't."

Q: *In the recent pro football draft, which I understood was mostly run by computers, do you know how much I.Q. had to do with each player's rating? Also, how did the teams get the I.Q. scores of the various players? —Clarice Benton, Cincinnati.*

A: A decidedly low I.Q. rating dropped a player at least one rung in all the pro computer ratings. "It's not what he can or can't learn about what is happening on the football field," an NFL exec explained. "It's that he may be more open to outside influences that can disrupt your team." The NFL clubs get most of their I.Q. data by having the players fill out questionnaires labeled "player aptitude test." Incidentally, there is a theory in the pros that super-high I.Q. is not desirable, either, especially at quarterback where a 125 rating is regarded as ideal.

Q: *Am I wrong, or hasn't my alma mater, Miami, produced more head football coaches, college and pro, than any other school? —Joe Sutherland, Dayton.*

A: Miami of Ohio had indeed produced more than a dozen head coaches, but this is a nearly impossible question to research completely. Until we hear differently, however, we will award Miami the palm for producing the most head coaches off one team. Sid Gillman's undefeated 1943 squad included Bo Schembechler, Paul Dietzel, Bill Arnsparger, and Ara Parseghian.

Q: *What is the origin of the shape of the football and the material it's made of? And what team was the first to use it? —Barbara McClintic, Salt Lake City.*

A: The original ball used, by Princeton and Rutgers in their so-called first game, was a pig's bladder covered with canvas. It was round, or as nearly round as they could get it. However, that actually was a soccer game. Later, McGill University of Montreal came south to play Harvard in 1874, introducing both Rugby Union rules and the rugby ball, which again was a pig's bladder covered with cowhide—in an oval shape. This was the ball that was adopted for the first rugby contests in the Ivy League, where American football evolved. Alonzo Stagg described this ball as "nine inches longer in circumference than the one we use now." And, of course, since Stagg the ball has been diminished to its narrow points, the better to throw, the poorer to kick.

Q: *What did the Oakland Raiders do, if anything,*

about their pom-pom girl who posed nude for Play-boy? —Connie Glueck, San Mateo, California.

A: They took her pom-poms away, but Jane Lu-beck had reached retirement age, twenty, on the job anyway before she became Miss September. The Raider organization stayed mum on the subject offi-cially, but they launched a furious investigation about who gave Jane the Raider helmet she used as a prop in the photos. Jane isn't telling, and they never found out, but she talks about the Raiders: "Their sex talk was very intense. They want this to be the first basis of a relationship. This didn't surprise me. They make it clear to you. Very clear."

Q: *During the hearings on the new gambling bill, the suspensions of Paul Hornung and Alex Karras came up again. I don't remember all the details, except that all either player did was bet on their own teams to win. I think one of Karras' bets was just a steak din-ner. Was there something else involved, or did Rozelle simply make an example of them? —Brent McManus, Athens, Georgia.*

A: There was little doubt then, and none today, that the action of Pete Rozelle in suspending Hornung and Karras for a year was justified. Gamblers look for angles. When an athlete bets on his own team, as they did, no matter how modest the amount, the word cir-culates. A few shrewd gamblers laid back and waited for the games Hornung and Karras did not bet on, then they went heavy for the other team. Inadvertently, the players were giving off signals that the Packers and the Lions were not confident about those games. We are told that by taking the opposition, often with points, a few gamblers that year cashed 70 percent of their bets, picking the games Hornung and Karras passed.

Q: *Would you be able to tell me the NFL require-ments which have to be met in order to obtain a franchise? I am a student at Boise State University and am doing research on the topic. —David A. Thomas, Boise.*

A: The last price for an NFL franchise was $16.5 million. The league bylaws specify that one man must own 51 percent of each franchise. This majority owner must also have some business ties in the area, to give the appearance of local ownership. He must submit financial statements to the league, which are thoroughly checked. Less publicized is the fact that the league also causes an investigation of the applicant's character and his social life. That's a pretty select club the owners are running.

Q: *I have heard a lot about the complicated rating system for pro quarterbacks and I would like to have some idea as to how it is done. —(No initial) Lesher, Germantown, Ohio.*

A: For the 1973 season, the NFL began a new system of ranking passers. Formerly, the system rated each passer against every other passer in a particular season. But this prevented a fan from knowing, say, whether Sonny Jurgensen had a better year in 1969 than Bart Starr did in 1966. So Don Smith of the Pro Football Hall of Fame and Seymour Siwoff, the statistical genius of the Elias Sports Bureau, worked out a permanent standard against which all passers could be measured. Smith and Siwoff arbitrarily decided to begin their gauge from the 1960 season.

There are four yardsticks—percentage of completions, percentage of touchdowns, percentage of interceptions, and average yards per attempt. The "average" performance since 1960 was found to be 50 percent completions, 5 percent touchdowns, seven yards average gain per attempt and 5.5 percent interceptions.

A complete rating table was printed. The rating points are then translated on the basis of 100, because that's a familiar numerical rating the fan can grasp.

With the new system, it's now possible to go back in NFL history and rank all players who ever threw the ball. The highest one-season rating was Milt Plum's

110.4 in 1960. Second was Sammy Baugh's 109.7 in 1945, followed by Bart Starr's 105.1 in 1966. The all-time passing leader (minimum, 1,500 attempts) is Len Dawson of Kansas City.

Q: *Some of us involved in a discussion believe you can answer this to our satisfaction. When did "redshirting" begin in the Big Eight Conference, the Pac-8, the Southwest, and the Southeastern?* —*Clyde Mc-Conner, Warsaw, Indiana.*

A: There have always been "redshirts," so-called because the scrub team that scrimmaged against the varsity wore red basketball jerseys over their practice uniforms. In the old days, when a player's eligibility was stretched by holding him out a season, it was invariably because he couldn't make the team and there was hope he'd develop later.

Redshirting as we know it today—stockpiling talented players according to the team's needs—began about 1947 when there was a crush of talent returning from World War II, colliding with the normal input of high school graduates. All the conferences you named have been redshirting ever since.

Q: *Can you tell me what became of Johnny Rodgers, the Heisman Trophy winner in 1972, and is there any truth to the rumors that he had some lucrative side deals while he was at Nebraska? A buddy of mine who went to Oklahoma heard that he did.* —*Chris Skinner, Little Rock.*

A: Rodgers was a star for the Montreal Allouettes for two years, having turned down an offer from San Diego to play in Canada. Your buddy's information is wrong, but could be based on a banquet joke told by Bob Devaney, the ex-Nebraska coach who recruited the widely sought running back.

Recalling that scene, Devaney said: "I put the grant-in-aid in front of him to sign. I told him, 'Now, Johnny, you'll get your tuition, your room, your board, your books, your laundry . . .'" Devaney noticed

35

Rodgers still held the pen in his hand but hadn't signed. "And so I added, 'Of course, Johnny, you understand that your laundry has the finest equipment and should net you a profit of $1,000 a month.'"

Rogers is back with San Diego.

Q: *I understand that Otis Sistrunk of the Raiders has worked with delinquents in Oakland. Can you tell me exactly what he did, and with what results, if any? —Ms. Dell Mendenhall, Riverside, California.*

A: With teammate Phil Villapiano, Otis counseled problem students, particularly those who were involved in vandalism. "Basically," explained Villapiano, "what we did was this. If anyone was caught damaging a bus, we put them in a room with Otis and they talked about it." School authorities say the property damage rate dropped noticeably.

Q: *I was shocked by the death of Em Tunnell, a great football player and a fine person. I saw him play as a rookie with the New York Giants, when he was still going both ways. He set records as a defensive back, but I always thought he would have been a great runner. I believe it was Steve Owen who switched him to defense. Am I right? —Carl Stout, Linden, New Jersey.*

A: Owen, the hefty coach of the Giants, went to some lengths to convince Tunnell that defense was more fun than running with the ball. "A little boy can carry a football," Owen once told him, "'cause it's real light." In time, Em came to the same conclusion: "Tackling is football; running is track." He was one of the NFL's pathfinders. When he reported to New York in 1948, he was the only black among fifty rookies.

Q: *I need a fast answer to a trivia question. My friend says a high school backfield in Pennsylvania once produced three college All-Americans in the same year. I need to know the players and their teams. —Mark Reeves, Tampa.*

A: In the mid-40s, Donora High School sent three backs on to college fame: Arnold Galiffa (Army), Deacon Dan Towler (Washington & Jefferson), and Bimbo Cecconi (Pitt). All made at least one All-American team, the Deacon winning small-college honors and going on to greatness as a pro. Donora, with a population then of under 10,000, also produced a fair baseball player named Stan Musial.

Q: *Who was the biggest man ever to play pro football?* —*Chip Crowell, Raleigh, North Carolina.*
A: Assuming you mean bulk, not length, your man would be Les Bingaman, the old Detroit Lions' middle guard, who was the subject of a curious bet in 1953. Buddy Parker, the Detroit coach, took one look at Bingo in camp and decided he must weigh 400 pounds. Line coach Buster Ramsey defended him, saying his weight was closer to 300. They wagered a steak dinner on it. When they tried to weigh him on a locker room scale, the overburdened machine just went "boinnnggg." Ramsey located a grain scale at a feed store, and Bingaman checked in at 349 pounds, eight ounces. Parker, a gracious loser, said his star lineman was in better shape than he thought.

Q: *Can you check this for me? Does George Halas, the owner of the Chicago Bears, hold the oldest record in the NFL books? If so, do you have any details?* — *Chris Bechtol, East St. Louis.*
A: Halas set the most enduring of all NFL records on November 4, 1923, when he ran 98 yards for a touchdown with a recovered fumble for the Chicago Bears. It was so long ago that Halas was chased by an Indian (Jim Thorpe, whose fumble he recovered, then with the Oorang Indians).

Q: *Now that a pro football team has hired a black head coach (Willie Wood of the Philadelphia WFL Bell), how long before some NFL team does it? Which club is most likely to hire whom?* —F. J. Kling, Chicago.

A: The first black head coach will probably be someone who is in the playing ranks now, such as Joe Greene or O. J. Simpson. Cleveland has to be the leading candidate because the Indians have already broken the ice. On this subject, the best statement was made by Jake Gaither of Florida A&M, the dean emeritus of black coaches: "If we consistently show ourselves to be good, to be efficient, to be alert and upward, and keep up with the game, I believe our country will eventually recognize us . . . So, just like it came about in basketball and eventually came about in baseball, it's going to come around in football. But it's going to be based on efficiency. Anything we get I want us to get because we're so darn good that they can't help but give it to us."

Q: *Can you give me a statistical rundown on the Georgia vs. Cumberland College game that ended 220 to 0? And how points were scored and score by quarters, etc.* —Bob Zimmerman, Houston.

A: First, it was Georgia Tech, coached by John Heisman, that laid it on disorganized little Cumberland on that October day in 1916. As you might imagine, the game was a statman's nightmare, and the details you want are not available. Suffice it to say that Tech scored every way a team can, leading at the end of the first quarter, 63-0. Cumberland had only sixteen players in uniform and the quarters were shortened to twelve minutes. The crowd on hand was estimated at 1,000 fans.

Q: *So many of my favorite pro football players are retiring, come to the end of the road, that I wondered if you knew what trouble they have "withdrawing" from the game. It seems like to me it would be rough coming down from the high of all that excitement every Sunday.* —Will Gordon, Salt Lake City.

A: We have talked to many ex-players and most

agree it's not the game itself they miss, but the association with their teammates, that feeling of being part of a group, with sometimes close dedication.

However, as the years go by, the action itself comes back into memory. Doak Walker, who quit the Detroit Lions in 1955, put it beautifully when he told writer Mark Goodman: "Miss it? Well, I'll tell you, when fall rolls around, and there's fresh-cut grass, and not quite frost, but you know it's coming, and there's that Evergreen liniment smell, and the smell of pads and leather, well my palms get awfully sweaty."

Cornell Green, who retired in 1975 from the Dallas Cowboys, says he had his own yardstick for retirement: "When you get too tired to go to the postgame parties on Sunday night. And Monday night."

Q: *The writers didn't give Terry Bradshaw a fair shake. They said the Steelers couldn't win with him in 1974 because he was dumb, but after six weeks on the bench he came back to lead them to the Super Bowl and he has taken charge again this year. Have any of the writers explained how he got so smart all of a sudden?* —Harvey Gennaro, Liverpool, Pennsylvania.

A: No, but one of his ex-teammates has a theory. Says Paul Martha: "Bradshaw had just been divorced, he was going bald, everybody was saying he was dumb. He looked the situation over and said, 'The hell with it. I'm just gonna play football. That's all I have left.' "

Q: *I know this question is asked all the time, but I have never yet heard an answer that I thought was satisfactory. When the Cleveland Browns lost their eighth straight game, one of the players said that all they had to play for now was their own pride. If it hasn't helped them up to now, why should it help in the rest of the games? Is that enough to keep a pro going, or is it the fear of losing their jobs that makes bad teams bear down in the final weeks?* —Arthur McInnis, Hiram, Ohio.

A: The best answer we've heard to this timeless

question came from Elvin Bethea, a fine defensive lineman who suffered through back-to-back 1-and-13 seasons in Houston. "It isn't pride that motivates a dog team," says Bethea, "It's anger. You're mad because the other guy is still coming at you hard. Mad at your wife because she's going to complain when you get home. Mad at yourself and the team and the fans because some of them got up and left at the half. And you're mad because you couldn't dress and leave with them. That's what you play on. Anger."

Q: *I missed seeing it myself, but my friends tell me Roger Staubach was on TV with Phyllis George and said something sensational about Joe Namath and sex. Can you find out how it went?* —*Charles Wentworth, Salt Lake City.*

A: Miss George, during Sunday NFL coverage on CBS, opened Roger's floodgates in a filmed interview by asking him how he got his reputation as a square. Staubach said it began when he chose a station wagon instead of a sports car after being named MVP of the Superbowl. He then complained, "I go to church on Sundays, so I am a religious fanatic." Finally, he remarked, "I probably enjoy sex more than Joe Namath. The difference is I enjoy it with one woman, my wife."

Q: *Can you tell me when the Super Bowl came to be called the "Super Bowl" and how?* —*Virginia Appleton, St. Louis.*

A: In the fall of 1966, six members of a "Merger Committee" met once a month and when the topic of The Game came up they didn't know what to call it. Lamar Hunt was a member of the committee, and it happened that his then eight-year old daughter, Sharron, was fascinated by a new toy, "Super Ball."

So one day at a meeting Hunt, almost unconsciously referred to the final game as the "Super Bowl." Soon all the committee members were using the term as shorthand for the "AFL-NFL World Championship," which is how the league officially referred to it for two years. But the wire services and *Sports Illustrated* picked up Hunt's phrase and it stuck. Now, don't ask us who first began counting I, II, III.

Q: *I am dating a man who says he is a pro football scout, whenever he comes through here. I want to know is he a scout and is he married? I called [the team] and they wouldn't tell me if he worked there, much less if he was single. Can you check this out for me? — (Name withheld), Norman, Oklahoma.*

A: You must get a high volume of traffic in scouts there in Norman. You note we have omitted all the names in your letter to protect the innocent. But, yes, your fellow is a full-time scout. And, no, we don't give out marital information, either.

Chances are, any pro football scout you ladies meet out there on the college trail is in one of three conditions: never been married, divorced, or separated in the process of. Some clubs, notably the Miami Dolphins, recognize a scout's job clashes with a home life, so they arrange that their men get home every other weekend. Miami's director of scouting is Bob Beathard, a divorced father of four.

Q: *It's too bad Paul Brown had to retire without getting his team into a Super Bowl. I think he could have made it if he hadn't traded Bill Bergey out of spite. Does Brown have any regrets about letting Bergey go? —Henry Sandifer, Cincinnati.*

A: Paul Brown never has any regrets. On the eve of the 1946 AAFC championship game, when his defensive captain was arrested for assaulting a policeman, Brown cut him from the squad. Jim Daniell never played another down of professional football.

As for missing the Super Bowl, Brown says: "The NFL championship game was OUR Super Bowl and we played in it seven times the first eight years in the league. And we won four straight in our old league before that. Perhaps all that doesn't count for much. It makes me sigh to think about it."

41

Q: *When are we going to hear more about the personality, anecdotes, etc., on Chuck Noll? At Green Bay, Miami, and even Dallas, the coach gets the credit. At Pittsburgh, the players get the credit. —Ace Devlin, Gainesville, Florida.*

A: Noll tries to turn aside any interview request: "Write about a player," he explains, "I'm not interested in publicity. It makes me uncomfortable. The only value I can see to being well known is financial and I'm not interested in merchandising myself. I'm a teacher. The important thing is my students."

Noll, in fact, is an interesting fellow of widely diverse interests, and in bygone days he would have been capsuled by the term "Renaissance Man." He is a gourmet cook and expert wine connoisseur, has a pilot's license, built his own stereo system, owns season tickets to the symphony, scuba dives for fun, photographs, and develops his own pictures.

Q: *The wife of a Dallas Cowboy said on TV that she didn't think it was a good idea for the wives to be with their husbands the night before the 1976 Super Bowl. If Dallas had it to do over again, would they keep them apart? —Jean Bergen, Grand Rapids.*

A: Tom Landry was asked at a press conference why he had departed from previous Super Bowl policy on this, and his answer, "Everybody likes a change now and then," brought down the house. Even Landry grinned when he realized what he said. And, yes, he'd do the same again, because Dallas players spent the night with their families before every home game this season. It really wasn't a change.

Q: *The song "Jamboree Jones" was sung by Andy Williams on the 1976 pre-game Super Bowl show, and I heard mention of Yale and the Rose Bowl. I know Yale never played in a Rose Bowl, but was the song written about a particular game? —John Grantham, Pekin, Illinois.*

A: Johnny Mercer wrote the ditty for Benny Goodman in 1934, but Goodman turned it down as being too Dixieland. It has since become a trivia standard with such singers as Mel Torme and Michele Lee. Mercer was inspired to write it when he heard the first collegian playing Dixieland in an SMU band solo during a game against Fordham in Yankee Stadium. The student was Eddie Green and the song was "Peanut Vendor." Green, now deceased, was a trumpet player, but Mercer changed Jamboree to a clarinetist, for Goodman.

Q: *Is Lou Holtz, who coached the New York Jets one year, related to the famous comedian of the same name from the 30s and early 40s? What other Jewish head coaches have there been in pro football? —Moise Bloch, Miami.*

A: Funny you should ask about the comedian. Jets' owner Phil Iselin had to break a luncheon date with director Mervyn LeRoy, visiting from the Coast, because of the press conference to announce the new coach. "Who is he?" asked LeRoy. "Lou Holtz," said Iselin. "You're crazy," LeRoy said. "Lou Holtz is eighty-three years old and the last time I saw him he was playing gin at the Hillcrest Country Club."

In fact, the Jets' coach was named after the comedian because he was dad Holtz's favorite comic, with his hilarious stories about Sam Lapidus. The only Jewish head coaches in the NFL we can remember are Sid Gillman and Allie Sherman. Incidentally, the Jets' Holtz is not Jewish.

Q: *Explain something to me. How much wild life can pro football guys get into on their road trips when they have curfews and room checks? —Larry K., Peoria, Illinois.*

A: Most NFL teams have 11:00 P.M. curfews and room checks on the road, but that doesn't mean opportunity can't knock at 1:00 A.M. It often does.

Q: *When the Browns hired Forrest Gregg as their*

new coach, somebody said that Lombardi called him the finest player he ever coached. I'm not putting down Gregg, but isn't that a little heavy for an offensive lineman? And what about Hornung or Starr? —Phil Appleby, Tampa.

A: It isn't likely that anyone could produce a tape recording of the voice of Vince Lombardi, who avoided such comparisons, singling out any of his players as Number One. But Gregg was one of his favorites, dating back to his willingness in 1961, at midseason, to give up his spot as an all-pro tackle and move in at guard to replace the injured Jerry Kramer. Vince also enjoyed the fact that Gregg admitted he liked to play in the mud. "It's kind of fun," the new Cleveland coach once said. "It gets in your mouth a little . . . but it seldom gets in your eyes."

Q: *Whatever happend to Joe Don Looney, the bad boy of professional football in the 1960s?—Harvey Sussman, Austin, Texas.*

A: Looney's mother tracked him halfway around the world and found him worshipping at a commune presided over by Swami Muktananda near Bombay, India. Joe Don rises at dawn each day for meditation and chanting, has embraced celibacy, vegetarianism, and temperance.

A gifted runner, Looney was with Detroit, Baltimore, and the NY Giants. He once broke up Johnny Unitas during a Colts pre-game prayer, when Unitas saw Looney back in the equipment room dancing the Mashed Potato. Looney liked to practice punting by seeing how high he could kick the ball straight up. After a good one, Looney would say, "How do you like that, God?"

Q: *Who in college football in 1971 was called the Italian Stallion? A friend says it was Ed Marinaro of Cornell and I stand firmly on Johnny Musso of Alabama. —Gary Paul S., Long Beach, California.*

A: You're right with Musso, the latest to have

drawn a nickname from the animal kingdom. Other notables: Alan (The Horse) Ameche of Wisconsin, Donny (Golden Palomino) Anderson of Texas Tech; and perhaps the most lyrically appropriate, Lance Alworth of Arkansas, known as "Bambi."

Q: *Don Rickles once said something hilarious about Bubba Smith and I can't remember the line. Can you?* —Eddie K., San Francisco.

A: Rickles said, "Bubba was on 'Wild, Wild Kingdom' once and they shot him."

Q: *Peter Gent's book "North Dallas Forty" has some awfully sleazy stories, supposedly about the Dallas Cowboys. How much of this stuff is on the level?* —Alex W., Los Angeles.

A: One-time flanker Pete Gent drew on his experiences with both the Cowboys and the Giants. Don Meredith, who inspired the character of the quarterback Seth Maxwell in the novel, confides to friends that "it is 90 percent true." Meredith jokingly refers to himself now as "Old Seth."

Q: *Who was the first black player in pro football, between Duke Slater and Joe Lillard? I said Duke Slater. I know Fritz Pollard was before them both.* — Hillary Hardison, Chicago.

A: Fred (Duke) Slater of Iowa, a tackle, played for the NFL Rock Island Independents in 1922, finished with the Chicago Cards in 1931. Joe Lillard, running back, Oregon, was with Chicago and Philly, 1932 and 1933. Pollard edged Slater for "first" by one year. After Lillard departed, the league had a "gentlemen's agreement" (apt phrase) not to sign any blacks. This lasted until 1946 when the LA Rams played Woody Strode and Kenny Washington, and the Cleveland Browns had Marion Motley and Bill Willis. George Preston Marshall at Washington was the last holdout, until 1962 when he traded for Bobby Mitchell. The

Redskins had a Southern TV network in the late 1950s, and the Redskin band played "Dixie" every Sunday.

Q: *Do pro football coaches ask the players, married or single, to abstain from sex before a game? If so, when does the countdown start?* —Helen K., Pittsburgh.

A: As you might imagine, the players' answers to this question vary. Said one Steeler, "Would you believe halftime?" But the norm is probably represented by Washington receiver Charley Taylor's wide-open reply: "My deadline is Thursday night."

Q: *Can you give me some information regarding the Outland Trophy awarded each year to the outstanding interior lineman in college football? Such as, the full name of the player who inspired this award, the college he attended, and the year it was first awarded?* —William G. (Bill) Outland, Lebanon, Missouri.

A: Your namesake was a turn-of-the-century Penn University great, John Outland, an All-American fullback in 1899 who moved to tackle on defense and played sixty minutes. The award was established in 1946 by the Football Writers of America, and the first recipient was the Notre Dame tackle, George Connor, later a pro standout with the Chicago Bears.

Q: *A guy offered to bet me that a former NFL official was involved in the Watergate case. Should I have taken his money?* —Anthony R., New York City.

A: He could claim a technical on you. William G. Hundley, one of the lawyers who represented John Mitchell during his Senate testimony, was once chief of the NFL securities division, investigating a reported fixed game in 1965.

Q: *I get it from a friend, a Democrat, that there is a football player in the past of Mrs. John Dean, the*

Watergate TV star. Who was (is) he? —Jack V., Dallas.

A: He was in football, but not as a player. For reasons of her own, the luscious Maureen kept secret her marriage to George Owen, then assistant general manager of the New Orleans Saints, when she filled out her marriage license application "at that point in time" with Dean.

Q: *Joe Garagiola had the Dodgers' third-base coach wired for sound for a TV game. I enjoyed it, but I wonder if this isn't an invasion of the game. They've done it in football, too. How can the coaches and managers put up with it? Don't they beef about it? —Jay Fawcett, Arlington, Virginia.*

A: The increasing investment of TV money in sports, and its relative importance to the budget, is forcing management to ignore tradition. This is a trend of the last five years. It reminds us of the time Vince Lombardi was astounded when a TV technician shoved a microphone into a sideline conversation the coach was having with his quarterback, Sonny Jurgensen. Lombardi roared: "You would stick that thing in a coffin!"

Q: *Pro football players pride themselves on playing with pain. The least little thing puts baseball and basketball players on the bench for weeks. Why can't they develop the same tough psychology? —Larry Farmer, Toledo.*

A: Even in the NFL, players at the skill positions can't play with pain. Also, toughness is often more real than apparent. Edward Vilella, star of the New York City Ballet, has been touted by sports-minded intelligentsia as the world's greatest athlete. They cite his leaping ability, his muscular physique and stamina. Furthermore, a medical survey disclosed that Vilella has ignored seven broken bones in his career. That's called dancing with pain.

Q: *There seems to be a rash of plays and movies*

about sports. I just saw The Championship Season *and I read that* Semi-Tough *is going to be a David Merrick musical. But all my life I've heard that sports was bad box office. What's happened?* —*Ellis K., Philadelphia.*

A: Until recently the last big show-biz success with a sports theme was the Broadway musical *Damn Yankees,* some twenty years ago. Playwrights and producers have rediscovered the dramatic content of sports. Dramatist Neil Simon has often incorporated sports into his hits (*Promises, Promises; The Odd Couple; Plaza Suite,* etc.). Simon says: "Sport is the only entertainment where, no matter how many times you go back, you never know the ending. In some ways basketball and football have the elements of farce. The main element of farce is timing. In a farce the characters always have the feeling that time is running out. In basketball and football time is always running out."

Q: *A honky I work with pretends to have no prejudice about black athletes. He says blacks are physically superior to whites and that's why they are going great. This sounds like a putdown to me. What are the facts and what do you think are the reasons the blacks are making it?* —*Henry Long, Washington, D.C.*

A: Blacks make up 10 percent of the U.S. population, 62 percent of the pro basketball rosters, 31 percent of the NFL, 34 percent of the National (baseball) League, 21 percent of the American. The physiological issue has been argued endlessly.

The Reverend Bob Richards, pole-vault and decathlon champion, has the best answer. "Two thirds of our Olympic team has come from the Negro race in the past. Why? Because the Negro has it tougher. He knows how to sacrifice." And, fortunately, the won-lost column is color-blind.

Q: *The great Philadelphia Eagles' running back [name withheld], was he white or Creole black?* — *G. L., Pekin, Illinois.*

A: In your terms, this is a lingering rumor, which is why we deleted the player's name and used only your initials. Your question also conveys a misconception about the term Creole, which actually means a French-Spanish mixture in old New Orleans society. However, such rumors have chased several famous New Orleans athletes and entertainers out of their hometown. Southerners call this "touched with the tar brush." New Orleanians say, "He has some coffee in his cream."

Q: *As a devoted soccer fan, I am not sure who got ripped off—the fans, the New York Cosmos, or Pele. I haven't read in any of the stories the fact that Pele rarely ranked among the leaders in goals in his last years with Santos. Given the limited popularity of the sport in this country, can he really be worth millions to play soccer? —Vincent Palafox, Tampa.*

A: Many years ago another Latin idol, Manolete, traveled to Mexico to receive the unheard-of price of $15,000 for each bullfight. The press was indignant. "Matador," a reporter asked him, "do you really propose to charge $15,000 for killing two bulls?" Replied Manolete: "I do not charge to kill the bulls. I charge to fill the plazas." Pele would be worth whatever the Cosmos paid—if he filled the plazas, and he certainly made a difference at the gate.

Q: *Could you straighten out something for me? I read a story not long ago that referred to the late Robert F. Kennedy as a "one-time star defensive player" at Harvard. I followed Ivy League football during the 1940s, which would have been his time, and don't remember it that way. Neither do my friends. Do you know how Bobby really ranked as a player? —Alton Kaine, Norwalk, Connecticut.*

A: Bobby Kennedy tried out for the Harvard team in 1945, spent most of that and the next season on the bench, but stuck it out and lettered on a weak Crimson team in 1947. One of the varsity managers of that squad, Dwight Nishimura, says of him: "He didn't make it because of any talent at defense. He didn't make it because he was so tough. He made it because of one quality . . . tenacity. No one worked as earnestly with less talent to make a team."

Q: *Can you tell me what athlete was the first to get big money from endorsements, a practice now carried to such extremes by Joe Namath? —Ms. Cheryl Perlman, St. Louis.*

A: Babe Ruth was among the earliest scorers with cigars and straw hats, but the first to find the mother lode was football great Red Grange, who was managed by the colorful C. C. (for "Cash and Carry") Pyle. In 1925, Grange endorsed hats, shoes, sweaters, dolls, and a soft drink. It nearly broke Pyle's heart when he had to turn down a lucrative offer from a cigarette company because Red didn't smoke. Later, C. C. observed that Grange could have been the perfect football player, if he had only learned to inhale.

Q: *I admire the way Kyle Rote, Jr., took his victory in the Superstars. I have been a long-time fan of Kyle Rote, Sr. He wasn't a Joe Namath playboy type, but I hear he was the model for the hero in a pretty revealing novel,* Only a Game. *Was he? —Henry Larrabee, Norfolk, Virginia.*

A: The book, written by ex-Giants publicist Robert Daley was reissued in paperback last year. It's no coincidence that the plot, about a running back's marital breakup, nearly paralleled the troubles of Rote, who got a divorce and married a one-time Miss America, Sharon Kay Ritchie. But the hero is reputedly a composite of Rote and teammate Frank Gifford.

Q: *In an underground paper, I read an interview with a Playboy bunny who told about dates with Mercury Morris and Joe Namath. Is this a put-on? —Norm Kelly, Chicago.*

A: A former Miami Playboy Club bunny, Samantha McLaren, supposedly from Danbury, Connecticut, is getting a lot of mileage out of her experiences with famous names. This is a new and scary trend in exploiting relationships with sports and show biz figures. It's getting so a fellow will have to make his date sign a loyalty oath promising not to write a book (*Upstairs with the Dolphins*). Samantha's claim to fame is based on a few dates with Morris when he was separated from his wife, and her roommate's one encounter with Namath. Joe was discovered to be "a very paranoid person, afraid that people were following him, listening at his door." Samantha's conclusion about athletes: "They are extremely gentle, and all biceps and triceps."

Q: *I keep hearing there is an underground, uh, chain of sports groupies. Well, I live in LA and would like to know where they hang out here, if any. —Ken Swarthout, Los Angeles.*

A: Well, the girls let it all hang out in LA at the Bull 'n' Bush, 3450 W. 6th Street. Tell 'em Joe Willie sent you.

Q: *On Monday Night Football, the network shows a movie of Alex Karras knocking down a horse by hitting him on the head. This isn't funny to me and I wish they'd cut it out. But anyway, did he actually knock down the horse? —Suzy Jacoby, Seattle.*

A: The stunt was done with wires that jerked the horse's feet out from under him, harmlessly, for the crazy movie, *Blazing Saddles*. Karras is zany enough himself, however, to try anything. During his suspension from the NFL for betting on his own Detroit team, Karras showed up at assistant coach Joe Schmidt's door one night selling Bibles. "I've got a Bible," Schmidt said. "Yeah," Karras said, "but this one's got a different ending." His most notable crack on Monday nights to date came when the camera focused on a lovely cheerleader. "That girl looks just like my wife," Karras said, "wants to look."

Q: *I read that the late poetess Marianne Moore once taught a class in which Jim Thorpe was a student. Can this be right? I always thought Thorpe went to an Indian school.* —Ray Engelman, St. Louis.

A: Thorpe, perhaps the greatest athlete who ever lived, took a course in commercial law from Miss Moore at the Carlisle Indian School in Pennsylvania. The subject seems out of character for both, but Miss Moore was a sports addict. "He was a gentleman," she once said. "I called him James. It would have seemed condescending, I thought, to call him Jim." Sports appeared in much of her poetry, including these lines of tribute to her favorite team, the Brooklyn Dodgers: "Getting better and better, zest, they have zest; Hope springs eternal in the Brooklyn breast."

Q: *Can you tell me who was the first black football player to win the Heisman Trophy and in what year? Also, how does the NFL justify the fact that it has never had a black head coach?* —Marshall Robinson, Seattle.

A: The late Ernie Davis of Syracuse, in 1961, became the first of his race to be honored as college football's player of the year. In answer to your second question, the NFL doesn't justify it. But there is a forgotten bit of league history that should be noted here. There was a black head coach in the early days of the NFL, Fritz Pollard, in the 1920s at Hammond.

Q: *I understand there is a new book out about the famous playoff game between the Colts and the Giants in 1958 and I am wondering if it is worth reading. What else is there left to say about that game? There must be at least a chapter on it in every pro football book written in the last twenty years.* —Eddie Cothran, White Plains, New York.

A: To write *Game of Their Lives,* David Klein revisited a host of Colts and Giants eighteen years after the first sudden death NFL title game. Partly to Klein's surprise, he plumbed depths of character in these men

52

to achieve a book unlike all the rest about pro football.

For example, Klein asked Kyle Rote if he thought he was hard to live with. The twice-divorced ex-Giant receiver looked around his newspaper-strewn apartment in Manhattan and said, "You don't see anybody else around here, do you? Must be. Must be."

Q: *There are several sports magazines that run a feature called "My Greatest Thrill" or "The Play I Remember Best" by different football players. As a nostalgia lover I always enjoy it, but I never see this done by coaches. I think that would be very interesting, if coaches like George Allen or Don Shula or Woody Hayes would reminisce about some of the famous moments in their career. How do I go about suggesting this? —Joseph Triola, Passaic, New Jersey.*

A: Just drop a note to the magazine of your choice, but don't hold your breath. Most coaches are consumed with thoughts of next week or next season, not the games of yesteryear. They either begrudge the time, routinely pass the request on to their team publicity man to answer, or do not take such things seriously.

A case in point is a long-ago poll of NFL coaches, who were asked to submit their favorite plays. Norm Van Brocklin, then with the Atlanta Falcons, wrote back: "My favorite play is *Our Town* by Thornton Wilder."

Q: *In 1975, Terry Metcalf of the Cardinals accounted for touchdowns in five different ways. Can you tell me what they were, and if this has been done before? —Oliver Berger, Landover, Maryland.*

A: Metcalf scored by rushing, receiving, returning punts and kickoffs, and throwing a touchdown pass. He was the fourth NFL player to accomplish this, the first since Gayle Sayers of the Bears in 1965. The others were Bill Dudley, of Detroit, in 1947, and George McAfee, Bears, 1941.

Q: *Can you tell me how the coaches actually send in plays from the bench? As complicated as most offenses are, how do the messengers remember all that stuff?* —*Neville Reinert, Richmond, Virginia.*

A: It isn't that complicated. The coaches just send in a number, say 38, and the rest is up to the quarterback. He has to decide which formation to use, which man to send in motion, and what the snap count should be.

Q: *A friend of mine seems to think that Notre Dame's Gus Dorais and Knute Rockne first introduced the forward pass to football. However I am a little older than he is and I know for certain that it was Eddie Cochems, then the coach at St. Louis University, who was the first. Please help me out.* —*Patrick J. Crowley, Davenport, Iowa.*

A: The forward pass had been used many times in college football before Gus Dorais and Knute Rockne hooked up in 1913. But the fact was, Dorais and Rockne put on their show at West Point, shocking a fine Army team, 35-13, before all of the high-powered Eastern press. Even though they did not invent the forward pass, the publicity traveled all over the country and they have been credited ever since with making the pass a football weapon.

In 1906 Wesleyan College put the ball in the air against Yale—Moore to Van Tassel—and for years that was considered the origin of the forward pass. But so many people have claimed to be the first that many sports encyclopedias no longer award that honor.

Q: *Now that Don Meredith is in movies, you hear a lot of crazy stories about things he did as a player. Is this just a legend being built up or, for instance, did Meredith ever actually sing in a huddle during a game?* —*Helen O'Connor, Butte.*

A: Most of the Meredith stories are exceeded in craziness and accuracy only by the ones you haven't heard yet. Yes, Meredith used to sing in the Dallas huddle. His favorite ditty was "I Didn't Know God Made Honky-Tonk Angels."

Says Meredith today: "Back when the Cowboys were going bad, a lot of our guys used to sing in the huddle. Then we started winning, and one day I realized I was the only one still singing."

Q: *One of the regulars on "Hawaii Five-O" is named Herman Wedemeyer. Do you know if he's the "Squirmin' Herman" Wedemeyer who played for St. Mary's in the mid-1940s? My wife and I saw him play against Fordham in the Polo Grounds in 1946. Thank you for any information. —E. H. Johnson, Texas City, Texas.*

A: It's the same fellow. Wedemeyer played high school football in Honolulu before going to St. Mary's, where he was an All-American halfback and took the Gaels to the 1946 Sugar Bowl, won by Oklahoma State, 33-13.

Q: *I understand that singer Jerry Jeff Walker was beaten up by a pro football player, but I have been unable to get the details. Can you find out? —Florence White, Tallahassee.*

A: The composer of "Mr. Bojangles" was almost a victim, but not quite. The TV snuff salesman, Walt Garrison, was with his wife and mother-in-law at a country-western nightspot when Walker began using intemperate language at a nearby table.

Garrison picked Walker up and pinned him against the wall, saying in his soft drawl, "I don't appreciate that kind of language around my family. If you don't clean up your act, I'll have to take you out in the alley and kill you." That was the end of the incident.

Q: *Is the quarterback in pro football eligible to be a pass receiver under any set of circumstances? I say he isn't. —Doyle Whittaker, Butte.*

A: In the 1950s, mainly because Bobby Layne worked the trick so well, the quarterback was made an ineligible receiver. The rule was later amended to say that if he put his hands under the center he was ineligible as a receiver—to prevent a play where the ball was snapped through his legs.

That's why today, before a quarterback shifts into a spread or shotgun formation, he keeps his hands at his side when standing behind center, so that he can be an eligible receiver. No one has tried it yet, however.

Q: *Do you have access in dollars and cents to any actual profit figures for the NFL teams? There are so many generalities and countercharges on this subject, I would like to know if there are any facts to go by.* —Everett Outlar, Butte.

A: The NFL Management Council, in figures certified by outside accountants, shows that the twenty-six NFL clubs in 1975 had an average profit of $384,000 on revenues of $7.4 million. That's a return of only 5.2 percent, which would have the average businessman perched on a ledge. The bottom eight teams, two of which lost money, earned an average of $266,000, for a return of only 3.1 percent. The teams, top or bottom, were not identified by name.

But it all shows you can't get rich running a pro football operation.

Q: *I am a high school player working out with my buddies for the coming season, and we have heard about some new "lean weight" program in professional football. Can you tell me what this is, and how can we get with it?* —Lon Whitley, St. Louis.

A: Several NFL teams are trying a new system to find out a player's "true playing weight." It involves weighing an athlete while suspended in a swimming pool up to his neck, then comparing this total with his regular weigh-in. The idea is that fat will float, but bone and muscle will not. The higher percentage of fat, the more weight he must lose.

Until now, "playing weight" has been decided arbitrarily by a coach's eyeball judgment. The NFL teams figuring "lean weight" will take another reading in mid-season, a final one in January, and then try to figure out what it all means.

Q: *In professional football, can you explain the terms Limbo and Cha-Cha? I am aware this has to do with the defensive linemen, but I am not sure how.* — *D. L. Kilpatrick, Grand Rapids.*

A: These are two-man games which can be put on at any time by the players themselves, in a pass-rushing situation. In a Limbo, the end will take the inside rush, and the tackle will rush the outside. A Cha-Cha is a similar stunt by the two tackles. Both terms, of course, originally referred to Caribbean dance steps.

Q: *I am trying to reaffirm a memory from World War II that an important bombing mission included a plane named in honor of Red Grange, the great Illinois halfback. Can you track this down for me, please?* — *H. D. Warren, Detroit.*

A: Grange recalls there was a B-25 bomber flying missions out of England, piloted by an Illini and named "The Galloping Ghost." Unknown to Grange there was also the incident of the B-29 which dropped an atom bomb on Nagasaki. This plane was named "The Great Artiste," but it was not painted on the fuselage. The only markings were the numerals "77," and Williams Laurence of the *New York Times* mentioned in his report of the bombing that this had been Red Grange's jersey number.

Q: *I have found a friend at [school deleted] whose marriage plans were postponed when her fiancé's football coach objected. I am wondering how widespread this practice is, and if the public realizes how much control coaches have over their players? I don't think we are naïve, but it seems so unfair.* — *(Name withheld on request)*

A: For years it was a rule at some schools—Ole Miss, for one—not to award scholarships to married players. That is no longer the case, but coaches, for reasons both selfish and practical, do not encourage players to marry before their senior years.

Explains Oklahoma's Barry Switzer: "Some of these young guys get married and later on down the line their wife's out working and they're hanging around the Union with all the pretty girls. It don't work. I've postponed a few of 'em . . ."

WINTER

Muhammad Ali dominated his stage as no man has since Edwin Booth dominated his. Since the mid-1960s, then, one question has haunted boxing: After Ali, what will be left? The deluge, probably. But some hope the answer will be George Foreman. In many ways Ali was larger than the sport; a Roman candle of a fighter. Foreman is an oak. He is a throwback, evenly drawn between Joe Louis and Sonny Liston. Moody, truculent, but with a decent streak. Street-tough, but often confused. Always with two new advisors who were going to straighten out his legal, personal, and romantic woes, just as soon as the suit was settled to decide which advisor had control.

George Foreman:
The Fighter

George Foreman's gym, way out in the piney woods outside of Marshall, Texas, is made out of red aluminum siding trimmed in white and is usually in cathedral silence because the ex-heavyweight champion of the world likes it that way. Whatever is Foreman's slightest whim becomes the firm dedication of everybody in his camp. There is no movement around the gym as he works out, and if anybody talks, they do so in whispers.

At the moment, Foreman is finishing up an after-lunch nap in one of the two rooms tucked under the loft, and Scrapiron Johnson is outside the gym door preventing trainer Charley Sipes' wife from swatting a chameleon. "Let it alone," he says. "It doing nothing. It don't even bite." He flipped it off a ledge and onto the grass. "Now, you watch. In a little while it turn green and you can't hardly see it. If it come out here on the dirt—where I'm standin'—it would turn brown. That's the way they do." He was explaining all this to a doubtful Mrs. Sipes and to Foreman's brother Robert, known as Sonny.

Scrapiron is one of Foreman's sparring partners. He is a short bull of a man who says he has had "about seventy-five or seventy-six fights," but the scar tissue around his eyes indicates a hundred would be closer to the total. In the parlance of the game he is a catcher, an "opponent" for fighters building a won–loss record. Now he is saying, "The doctor told me to stay out of it. I woke up spitting blood." Foreman had caught him the day before with a left hook to the chest bones, where they meet just above the stomach. "It wasn't a hard shot," he said. Scrapiron has never been hit hard in his life, by his reckoning. "But it was a clean shot, like a fighter do when he gets his timing together."

Sonny Foreman is sitting on the steps to the gym, below a sign that says "George Foreman's School of Hard Noks." He says, "That's right. George isn't getting mean, maybe a little irritable, but he's sure getting into form. That right he hit John Adams didn't travel this far, and it broke three ribs." Adams had also been a sparring partner, and now the only one left is Bob Stallings, another short and wide heavyweight who hooks with both hands.

Foreman was being trained against this style of fighter, of course, because he wants an approximate imitation of Joe Frazier, the man he would fight that Tuesday night on national theater television, out of the Nassau County Coliseum in New Jersey. It was to be the next step in his pursuit of the Holy Grail, a rematch with Muhummad Ali, the man who embarrassed him and knocked him out in Zaire, Africa. He would demolish Frazier and end his career.

Lamar Davis, one of Foreman's "countless cousins," is at the gym door. "Everybody come in now," he says. Foreman has come out of his lair, the only way to put it, and is easing himself through the ropes into the ring at one end of the building. He motions to Sonny, and Sonny hurries to the tape deck and speakers along one wall to click on an album of Aretha Franklin's spirituals, "Amazing Grace." This tape will play over and over and over during the next hour and a half. Alone in the ring, Foreman goes into a slow straightforward shuffle, throwing short jolting punches which ripple the powerful muscles across his shoulders. When his movement takes him near the ropes, he does a sharp left flank and keeps on.

Foreman, at 6–3 and between fights as much as 240, was the largest heavyweight champion since Primo Carnera. As he moves now, punching at the air, he seems a mountain of a man, slim-hipped, long-legged, with biceps no larger than a small child's waist. He is completely expressionless and intent. He motions Sonny to jump the Aretha Franklin tape, and when the sister starts hitting a faster beat he steps up his pace.

Henry Winston, Foreman's "manager of the moment," begins a low conversation in a far corner of the gym. Winston, a sharp and nervous fellow out of Oakland, where he used to promote fights, tells people he is Foreman's manager, with the proviso "of course, George might fire me tomorrow." Foreman says Winston is his assistant and "I have a lot of assistants."

"He's like Sonny Liston," Winston is saying, referring to the late ex-heavyweight champion who "gave" a young Cassius Clay the title. "He's withdrawn, likes a lot of privacy, he's never boisterous. But he's kind if he likes you. It's either that or he dislikes you. His left hand is the reincarnation of Liston's left hand, the same kind of power. And he has his own way with it. He'll shoot the left and it's not pepper, shoot it again and it's still not pepper, then maybe the third time it's a stinger. And when he steps in behind it and does this"— Winston brought his left arm up in a tight uppercut— "there's no man alive who won't drop." Winston had only been Foreman's manager for three months, but by now the two of them could whip anybody in the world.

Foreman is working with the gloves on against his trainer, Sipes, who once was the welterweight champion but has since acquired an enormous pot belly. Sipes has his forearms taped with Holiday Inn towels because they have become bruised and swollen from other sessions against the big man. Sipes imitates Frazier's hooking, boring-in style very well, and he's trying to get Foreman to do a couple of things: Keep his glove on either side of his chin, his arms protecting the body, elbows in, and still counter with a short left after taking a right-hand shot. The accent is on keeping the punches short. "You can do as much good from in here," Sipes says, "as from way out there," imitating one of Foreman's care-free punches.

Then Sipes says, "Oh, my God, you hit me in the tummy." He went over and leaned against the ropes, laughing in pain. For the first time, Foreman was laughing, too.

"He is training as much for Ali as for Frazier," Winston says. "He won't have any problem finding Frazier. You don't need any binoculars to find Joe Frazier. If you can find your chest, you got no problem, because that's right where he's gonna be. He is on railroad tracks, coming straight at you. If anybody could design a perfect opponent for George, Joe would be it. When he came back to the dressing room after knocking out Frazier in Jamaica, for the title, his right-hand glove had Frazier's teeth marks on it. George hit him so hard he split Joe's mouthpiece, which is as thick as a horseshoe, and got to the teeth."

Sipes is now working on another stratagem, where he comes in low à la Frazier, and Foreman ends up laying his weight across his back with "Frazier's" head tucked into the Foreman belly. Foreman lays on his back until Sipes cries uncle, and Foreman laughs again. "That's 240 pounds you got on you," Foreman says.

Winston addresses himself to the subject of what the hell happened to Foreman in Zaire. "He got the eye cut which caused a month postponement in the fight," Winston says. (He was there as a spectator.) "And the layoff staled him. He didn't like the climate or the water, and the surroundings bored him. Also he got the wrong food served to him, which is what I think was the big thing, and when he came into the fight his body salt content was so low he didn't have any energy. When he came back from the first round he was so tired he was cross-eyed. The world didn't see the real George Foreman in that fight."

It was suggested to Winston that Ali had a home-court advantage roughly equal to the time Battling Siki lost his light-heavy title to Mike McTigue on St. Patrick's Day in Dublin. On a decision.

"If George had won a decision in Zaire," Winston said, "there would have been a Mau-Mau riot. Ali came into the ring and he timed it so he waited until George was coming down the aisle, then he got the crowd to start chanting: 'Ali, boom-eye-aye.' Translated that means, 'Ali, kill the blankety-blank.' "

Winston held a belief that it was only a matter of time before Foreman got his rematch with Ali. He was waiting on a call which he hoped would tell him that Ali had decided to give Foreman "Ken Norton's date" in September, because Ali had a movie scheduled in October and that would mean a spring, 1977, delay for Foreman. (This hope was short-lived. Ali fought Norton in September in Yankee Stadium, and won a hotly disputed decision.) "Herbert Muhammad [Ali's Muslim manager] is going to make him fight George again," Winston said, "because there's nowhere else he can get that kind of money in one shot."

Indeed, there are a lot of people who would have been delighted to see George obliterate Ali, he of the wide and highly operative mouth, but fight fans grudgingly agree that there would not be many people at all who thought about boxing, a fading sport, had it not been for the controversial champion from Kentucky. Still, George Foreman has the moment etched in every sports fan's eye, when he paraded around the ring with a tiny U.S. flag clutched in his massive fist after winning the 1968 Olympic championship. Those were the Games in Mexico when other black winners had lifted black-gloved fists on the victory stand. And America has never forgotten it. There was also Foreman's repeated gratefulness to the Job Corps, a J. F. Kennedy program, for getting him out of a Houston ghetto and into the straight side of life. It was while he was in the Job Corps that he was induced to become a boxer.

It can't be said that Foreman had a checkered childhood in Houston. There was nothing checkered about it—it was all black squares. There were two families in his neighborhood who owned television sets. His first ambition was to be a defensive tackle for E. O. Smith

Junior High School. "The way I was, for me to learn I had to get the attention of the teacher," Foreman has said, "and there were other kids who were always better at that, so I didn't get the attention of the teacher, and I didn't learn. That took care of football. I dropped out in the ninth grade." (Oddly, other great athletes short on education have lodged a similar complaint. When hockey star Gordie Howe came home crying after flunking the third grade two years in a row, his mother asked him why he didn't get help from the teacher, and Howe said, "I didn't want to bother her, mum.")

For the next few years Foreman hoisted hubcaps, rolled winos, and used the money to drink cheap wine himself. Finally, he and a friend joined the Job Corps, just to get out of town for a vacation. All his fellow corps-mates began calling him "Big George" and telling him he ought to be a fighter. He took their advice.

Now he is working hard against Bob Stallings, both fighters wearing massive leather cups to protect the groin, and headgear and sixteen-ounce gloves. Sipes is urging Foreman to rough Stallings up with his hands, not as a boxer but as a wrestler. At times Foreman gets a headlock on the shorter Stallings. Again he will put both hands behind Stallings' neck and pull him across the ring and into the ropes. Clearly, the Foreman camp intended for their man to manhandle Frazier.

Foreman had been in daily training at his piney woods site for more than three months. Since there had been a paternity suit recently lodged against Foreman ("Harassment" is the official explanation), Winston was asked what Foreman did for female companionship way out there in the country. "He does all right," said Winston.

Foreman is working five hard, three-minute rounds with Stallings, and in the fourth he was up on his toes dancing to his left and flicking out the jab, a simulated Ali floating like a bee and staying away from Frazier's left hook. He looked like an elephant drinking tea out of a china cup.

Foreman next turned to the exercise mat to do sit-ups, and Stallings strolled over, no wetter than an Hawaiian surfer. "How's he hitting 'em?" Stallings was asked.

"I don't hear so good just now," Stallings said grinning. "He got me a shot to the head. I think he's getting anxious to fight." Stallings, out of New York, scored an upset over contender Ernie Shavers in 1974 and hasn't been able to get a fight since. Shavers has, but not Stallings. "George doesn't have any reason to worry about Frazier," he said. "Frazier is made for Foreman. But Ali will never fight George. You can say a lot of things about Ali, but one thing he isn't—he's no fool. I don't care what the money is. Ali is through. He'll never fight anybody hard. It will be worth more money and prestige to him the rest of his life to retire undefeated than if he was to get stopped by Foreman." (He was correct on the Frazier half of his prediction. And no Ali fight was in sight when 1977 began.)

Foreman has gone to the shower. A videotape camera recorded all his sparring with Sipes and Stallings, but he won't look at the replays today, Sonny Foreman explains, because he doesn't consider them meaningful. Sonny is outside the gym, gazing across a huge water tank which Foreman calls "my lake." This is a fifty-five-acre estate the fighter has purchased, including a hayshed, stable, three-bedroom brick home in the distance, and a newly built set of cages and animal houses. Foreman has thirteen horses, fifteen dogs, one lion, and one tiger. Mornings before ten he will roughhouse with the lion, whom he regards as "just like me."

Sonny says his brother bought this place because he was born in Marshall, in a house alongside the Oak Grove Baptist Church "up along possum ridge." Sonny says, "I don't know how he stands it, staying out here all the time. He'd be content to never leave. Me, I was born in Marshall, too, but I have to see some bright lights *once* in awhile. It just suits him. When he was training for the Ron Lyle fight it seemed like things weren't just right. There was something missing, as if

George was uncertain of himself. Now things are swinging back to what they was before."

Foreman emerged from his back door of the gym, looking sleek and slender in a white T-shirt, slacks, and sandals. He posed casually for two photographers, one from the German magazine *Stern*.

The bitterness of losing the championship has seemed to temper Foreman into an adult. It is as if, at age twenty-seven, he has at last lost his baby fat, both physically and mentally. He stands there "very confidential" as he fields one question after another.

"I never got used to not being the champion," he says. "I still ain't used to it and never will be. It's all I think about every minute I'm training. That's why I work so hard, and that's why I'll be champion again, because nobody works harder than me."

Foreman talks softly but with ample volume as he slides over all the hard consonants in a sentence. "I don't have anything against Ali, even though he's going around fighting a bunch of nobody people instead of fighting me again. Ali kept the game alive, the way I look at it, and credit to him. Going to fight that Japanese wrestler is bad—but I did something just as bad fighting those five guys in Canada. Otherwise, he hasn't hurt boxing at all."

The big fellow ambles down to the stables at the request of the photographers—they require a bigger animal prop to put this man in perspective—and he reins a honey-blond horse through the gate, warning the bystanders, "Watch it, keep clear, this is a stud." Foreman says the horse is a Tennessee Walker that has spoiled him for all other horses. "It's like sitting in a rocking chair to get on him," he says, "and the other horses I got jolt my insides out." He believes in quality animals; his three German shepherds are thoroughbreds from Germany at $4,000 each.

"I am for sure a country boy," Foreman says. "If I didn't have to make money, I would never leave here. I wish I could fight on the dirt right outside my gym and never have to ride an airplane."

Foreman's end of the Zaire fight was $5.6 million, and his people believe he perhaps banked $2 million of it. He collected a flat $1 million from the Frazier fight, but he has a way of finding a place for it all—a $56,000 Rolls Royce, a Mercedes, a custom Cadillac, a mobile home for privacy from his family, a home in Marshall for his mother, a payroll of eighteen relatives and close friends. Foreman is cozier than Ronald Reagan when asked for a general statement of his finances. "I'm still working," he says, "so I'm still spending. If I had to stop working, then I'd have to worry about what I was spending."

Once he told Roger Kahn of *Esquire* magazine: "Internal Revenue is the real undefeated heavyweight champ. They show you the left. You never see the right. They'll take everything, even your tears."

He is far enough away from Zaire now to put it in his own terms. His off-the-cuff explanation of his kayo by Ali: "I used the wrong strategy from the first round to the last. But you've got to credit Ali. He withstood the pressure I put on him."

In a deeper vein he blames the eye that forced a month's delay. "I had never been cut before," he says. "And what my people didn't understand was, that cut was an illness that needed to be healed mentally. Another thing, you ever have the feeling you couldn't leave a country? I wanted to go to Paris to see a doctor for treatment of the cut, but suddenly all of the airplanes in Africa were out of business. When I went back to training for the fight, I couldn't spar. How are you going to get ready for a fight if you can't work out? I'm going to prove to the world that wasn't George Foreman they saw that night."

Someday, he thinks, there will be Ali. "Pressure will make Ali fight me," Foreman said. "The people in boxing will put up the bread—they want something big. Some people say Ali has gone back [Foreman must have been talking to Stallings] but I don't care about that. Whether he's at his peak or gone down, I'll take him. A man who does the work—spars, runs, boxes, punches the bag—there comes a time when he hits a peak. Well, the harder he works, the longer he stays at a peak. Now maybe Ali is beyond that. I will leave it for other people to figure out. I don't give a damn."

Come to think of it, Sonny Liston trained to Count Basie's "Night Train." It's eminently fitting that Foreman trains to "Amazing Grace."

Questions & Answers

Q: *Watergate Judge John Sirica is pictured as a longtime friend of Jack Dempsey. Is Sirica just a celebrity hound like so many other people?* —*Anthony Conforto, Baltimore.*

A: Sirica is a cut above a celebrity hound. He is a nostalgic ex-pug, a man of achievement and forceful personality, thus well qualified to be friends with the great Dempsey, who served as best man at Sirica's wedding. Sirica was once the sparring partner of welterweight champ Jack Britton in the 1920s, and also fought semifinals on Miami fight cards. The Miami boxing writer of the day termed him "a great little mitt artist." Sirica paid his way through law school as a boxing coach at the Washington, D. C., Knights of Columbus at $100 a month.

Q: *I just saw the TV movie,* Great White Hope, *and want to know how closely it stuck to the real facts of Jack Johnson's career—was his trouble caused by a white woman and did he throw the title to Jess Willard?* —*Andrew T. Holt, Louisville.*

A: Jack Johnson, whom the late Nat Fleischer rated the greatest of all heavyweights, had two interracial marriages. In a prelude to the first marriage, he was charged with violation of the Mann Act, jumped bail, and went to France. The movie was true in theme, but not detail, to the tragic career of Johnson, who knew that white fight fans would hate him no matter what he did.

He was thirty-seven and out of condition when he lost in the twenty-sixth round to Willard in Havana, taking the count with a glove over his eyes to shield away the sun. Moments before, he had his manager tell his wife to leave the arena. Johnson knew when he accepted the match he would be giving up the title, because he was too far past his peak to beat young Willard over a forty-five-round distance—actually a fight to the finish. He lost the way Sugar Ray Robinson "lost" to Joey Maxim, from exhaustion. After the fight, he said, "Now all my troubles will be over. They will let me alone." But Johnson fought three more years out of the U. S., then came home to accept a prison term in Leavenworth.

Q: *I saw your column in the Chicago paper. The people in sports up here won't answer questions. Can you tell me—wasn't the Louis-Conn fight scheduled for twenty rounds? And what was the longest fight in history? —Ed Smallwood, Toronto, Ontario.*

A: You got part of it right. The last heavyweight title fight scheduled for twenty was Joe Louis–Bob Pastor in Detroit, 1939. Louis KO'd Pastor in eleven rounds. Longest glove fight was between Andy Bowen and Jack Burke, middleweights, 110 rounds to a draw, in New Orleans, 1893. Elapsed time was seven hours, nineteen minutes.

Q: *When boxing people rate the great heavyweights they seem to skip over Rocky Marciano to talk about Louis and Dempsey and Jack Johnson. The Rock had one thing all those guys didn't. He never lost a fight and he fought everybody. Don't you agree he was the best? —Martin George, Louisville.*

A: We're on your side that nobody, but nobody, could have withstood Marciano's assault in his prime.

But the Rock was shortchanged by events. He started too late and retired too soon, with a 49-0 record. Ted Williams says, "He should have had one more fight. Nobody would ever forget 50 and oh."

Q: *Was Rocky Marciano ever knocked out?* — *Charley Everts, Brockington, Massachusetts.*

A: This is a tricky one you can take to your favorite barroom. The record book says no, but the Rock said yes—for about six seconds in the first round of his first fight with Joe Walcott. But he came around and upright within ten and took Walcott out in the thirteenth.

Q: *Has there ever been a father and son combination in boxing?* —*Gary Kanka, Harrison, New York.*

A: There have been thirty-nine father-son combinations in the ring through the years, including Bob Fitzsimmons and Junior. The most effective duo was Jack Britton and son Bobby. Papa was welterweight champion. Bobby was a welterweight contender.

Q: *Can you tell me how old Sugar Ray Robinson was when he retired?* —*Roosevelt Anderson, Passaic, New Jersey.*

A: Walker Smith, as Sugar Ray, is generally acknowledged the greatest boxer-puncher the fight game has ever known. He was born in Detroit in 1920, retired the first time in 1952, made a living in nightclubs as a dancer, and had his last fight, an exhibition, at age forty-two.

Q: *There was a middleweight fighter out of France, by the name of Marcel Cerdan. It has been said that he was on his way to regain the title from Jake La-Motta at Madison Square Garden in New York. I'm sad to say that he never arrived, as his plane crashed. When, and where, did the plane crash and was his body ever recovered? —Antone A. King, Jr., Riviera Beach, Florida.*

A: Marcel Cerdan, one of the romantic figures of boxing legend, was born in Casablanca, French Morocco. He won the middleweight title from Tony Zale in September of 1948, lost it a year later to LaMotta in Detroit, by a knockout. Flying to this country for a return match, he died in a plane crash over the Azores on October 27, 1949.

Handsome, with dark, curly hair, Cerdan was jeered in his first appearance in front of an American crowd when he entered the ring (against Georgie Abrams) in a baby blue bathrobe. But he became as great a favorite here as in Europe, and the country mourned his death. His body was never recovered. Cerdan was the lover of the famed French singer Edith Piaf.

Q: *A dealer at the Desert Inn in Las Vegas told me Sonny Liston used to be in the casinos every night. Was he a heavy gambler? Did Liston die broke? — Randy Brickman, Scottsdale, Arizona.*

A: (1) Whatever Liston was addicted to, it wasn't gambling, and (2) he left no large debts. Sonny simply enjoyed the movement, the excitement of the casinos.

A friend tells a story about the ex-heavyweight champion's style at the blackjack table. The dealer asked if he wanted a hit. "What you got in the hole?" asked Liston, outraging every rule of the game. The dealer told him to take a card or fold. Whereupon Sonny reached across the table, turned over the dealer's hole card, then said, "Okay, hit me." He lost.

Q: *Is the girl who is supposedly writing a book about Jack Dempsey really his daughter? If so, how objective can it be? When will it be published? —John Shisken, Binghamton, New York.*

A: Barbara Dempsey, twenty-five, is the daughter of Jack's fourth wife. She is blond, attractive, and bright, speaks five languages. Her book about her stepfather, she says, will be "positive and admiring." It is about one-fourth finished and no publication date has been set. Unresolved is how Barbara will handle such sensitive matters as the old heavyweight champ's first marriage to a lady he met in an assignation house on Commercial Street in Salt Lake City.

Q: *I saw Joe Louis referee the Frazier-Quarry fight and it reminded me that nobody ever ruled the title the way he did. I think I could prove it if I had the figures. I don't believe he ever had a championship fight where he was less than a 3-1 favorite. Am I right? —Pat Langham, Memphis.*

A: Only three times was Louis less than 3-1 the day of the fight. In the second Schmeling fight he was 9-5, in the second Billy Conn fight 14-5, and in the second Joe Walcott meeting 13-5. In all other title bouts he was never less than 5-1, and frequently 20-1. Before Louis such odds in heavyweight title fights were a rarity. Jack Dempsey, for instance, was only 3-1 over Georges Carpentier and Luis Firpo.

Q: *The fact that Joe Louis is employed as a "greeter" by a Las Vegas hotel, isn't this the most shameful use of an ex-heavyweight champion, especially a great one like Louis? —Eddie O., San Francisco.*

A: Louis was indeed a great one, not only in the ring. As New York Mayor Jimmy Walker said, "He laid a rose on the tomb of Abraham Lincoln." But, no, the most shameful use of the champ was by Jimmy Hoffa in his bribery case in 1957. The FBI thought it had an open-and-shut conviction, but Joe Louis made conspicuous appearances in the courtroom where he made a great show of affection for the Teamsters chief. A jury of eight blacks and four whites acquitted Hoffa.

Q: *In my opinion, Muhammad Ali is the most obnoxious person the fight game has ever known. It's too bad that Jack Dempsey or Joe Louis aren't around*

74

to shut his big mouth once and for all. I think every one of his fights is nothing more than the perpetration of fraud on the fight fans. The way Howard Cosell touts him leads me to believe he has a piece of the action. Is this true? —Elmer Massing, Interlachen, Florida.

A: This is the irony of their relationship. Although the public thinks of them as a kind of nightclub act, few have been wrong about Ali more often than his friend Cosell. Howard thought Sonny Liston would destroy the young Cassius Clay. He said Ali was washed up after the loss to Joe Frazier. And with great finality, he predicted that "Ali will never touch George Foreman, vocally or otherwise." Yet through the years, they helped make each other rich and more famous. From the beginning, says Howard, Ali "sensed that the two of us made a very good pair in reaching the public."

Q: *Can you find out the truth about the real relationship between Howard Cosell and Muhammad Ali? Do they like each other, hate each other—or do they use each other as an act? —Ben Blair, Des Moines.*

A: There is a genuine feeling between Ali and Cosell that dates back to their first encounters. What Ali will always remember was that Cosell was the first public figure to approve his right to change from Cassius Clay to a name in the Muslim faith. Cosell later was practically alone in outrage when the New York Boxing Commission took away Ali's title. The Boca Grande of ABC was attacked as a "white Muslim." Cosell on the other hand is genuinely fond of Ali. And each knew instinctively that they made for good show biz.

Q: *Muhammad Ali makes a big to do about his Muslim wife and his Muslim life. What happened to his first wife? Did she decline to adopt his faith? —Beatrice Leigh, Omaha.*

A: Ali has often listed among his sacrifices "the pretty little girl" he gave up for the Muslims. Sonji

Clay, as she was known in those days, never did accept the Muslim mode of dress and other restrictions, but that wasn't the cause of their breakup. Sonji had been a professional model and knew her way around the sports and social whirl.

Q: *Muhammad Ali was on TV before the Ali–Foreman fight and gave a terrific answer when the interviewer asked how he'd like to be remembered. I have tried to tell my friends about this, but I can't get how he said it. Would appreciate it if you can somehow find this and reprint it in the paper. —Coley Stein, West Palm Beach.*

A: David Frost was the interviewer on CBS and here is Ali's reply: "I'd like for them to say, he took a few cups of love. He took one tablespoon of patience. One teaspoon of generosity. One pint of kindness. He took one quart of laughter, one piece of concern, and then he mixed willingness with happiness. He added lots of faith, and he stirred it up well. Then he spread it over a span of a lifetime and he served it to each and every deserving person he met."

Q: *I read where Ali has two Rolls Royces, a bus, a Cadillac, and a couple of antique cars, and he buys them the way some people buy ice cream. Is he crazy, or does he just like cars? —Hayden Knox, Sacramento.*

A: Cars have become a symbol to fighters and Ali explains it: "All fighters when they come into money, first thing they do is get 'em a couple of nice cars. Ain't nothing wrong with it. I had raggedy cars all my life. Joe Louis liked to drive. Jack Johnson drove everywhere. Jack Dempsey, Ezzard Charles, Sugar Ray . . . prizefighters like to feel the wheel in their fists and a motor underfoot."

Q: *What I never understood was why didn't Muhammad Ali go into the Army when he knew they would never put him near any live bullets but would*

trot him around like all the other aces they've had?
—Roosevelt T., Tampa.

A: At the time Muhammad failed to take "one step forward," he had been offered a deal by the Army that was even softer than the one Joe Louis had in WW II. The champ would have been assigned to Special Services for USO-type tours, with a provision for title defenses. But his Muslim advisors insisted he become a martyr.

Q: *Settle a bet. Did Muhammad Ali ever serve even one hour behind bars when he had trouble over the draft evasion? —Jerry P., Detroit.*

A: Not for draft evasion. But Ali did make it for three days in Florida when arrested for driving without a license. Ali says the judge told him: "Get your tail . . . ready for jail . . . without no bail."

Q: *As I get it, Ali and Frazier blew their big money match because they couldn't agree on a split of the purse. This got me wondering. What's the smallest paycheck in a heavyweight title bout? —Tony Camarata, Louisville.*

A: Zero dollars. In the last winner-take-all title fight, James J. Corbett kayoed John L. Sullivan for the $25,000 purse and a $10,000 side bet. The old champ wound up with nothing.

Q: *Frazier claimed that Ali once asked him for a job when he was having his problems with the draft. Is there any truth to that? I can't believe Ali would humble himself like that. —Isaac Scott, Decatur, Illinois.*

A: In the fall of 1970, when Joe was champ and he was still in limbo, Ali suggested that he be hired to spar with Frazier IF his license to fight was not restored. Frazier took the offer seriously. The best guess is that Ali was either testing Joe or curious to get in a ring with him and size up the man he expected to someday meet for the title. The idea intrigued Frazier, who asked Ali how much pay he'd want. Joe lost interest when Ali said "a couple hundred a week." Though they were to fight for millions, he thought that was too much to pay a sparring partner.

Q: *After himself, who does Ali consider the greatest heavyweight of all time? And how does he feel about Rocky Marciano beating him in that computer TV fight of a few years ago?* —C. J. Merrick, Austin.

A: Ali's choices for place and show are Joe Louis and Jack Johnson. Based on movies he has seen and what he has been told by old-timers of that era, he rates Marciano behind Jack Dempsey and Gene Tunney. (He believes that Marciano and Joe Frazier, both in their prime, would have been a match.) As for the computer fight, he dismisses the outcome airily: "You KNOW that was a fake. Whites wanted to see Marciano go down as the greatest heavyweight of all time. When he wasn't."

Q: *Why all the buildup and hullabaloo for Mr. Ali? Young sportswriters get the impression he invented boxing. Joe Louis not only beat more champs, but kayoed them—Carnera, Baer, Schmeling, Sharkey, Braddock, Walcott. He never avoided any man as Ali has done. Louis never fought any exhibitions. Rocky Marciano used to beat people so bad they had to quit fighting (Charles, Walcott, Louis). Ali never did this. He may be the greatest boxer in heavyweight history, but not the "Greatest Champ," like he brags.* —Sam Fanuzzi (no return address).

A: About Louis, his handlers did avoid a return with Max Schmeling, until after Joe had won the title from Braddock, a match the German had been promised. The delay of two years was crucial to the thirty-five-year-old challenger. Louis fought 111 exhibitions from 1945 to 1951.

Fight experts generally agree that Ali ranks with Jack Johnson and Gene Tunney as the best "boxers" in the division's history. Louis was the best boxer-puncher, Marciano the greatest puncher, and Ali the "fastest" heavyweight of all time.

Q: *You hear some wild tales about Derek Sanderson, the hockey star, but this tops them all. My boyfriend says Derek made a porno movie a couple of years ago. Is that a put-on, or did it happen? If so, is the movie showing anywhere?* —Angie Sapinsky, Detroit.

A: This requires a little explaining, as Sanderson's exploits often do. The truth is, the moustachioed ex-Bruin, ex-Ranger was nearly the dupe of a clever promotion scheme by a Montreal filmmaker. Derek was given a small part in a movie, playing a hockey coach. He attends a party where the leading lady meets and flirts with him, all very innocent.

When Sanderson and his attorney attended a private showing of the movie, they discovered that his was the only clean scene in the picture. It was indeed a porno flick. The promoters had planned to exploit Sanderson's name in their advertising. His attorney wasted no time in getting his scene edited from the film and, alas, Derek became another face on the cutting room floor.

Q: *Gordie Howe and the other players for Team Canada complained about their treatment in Russia, and Howe said his room was bugged. What I want to know is, what could Howe possibly say that would interest the Russians?* —Lou Covington, Atlanta.

A: Invasions of tourists' privacy in Russia are often more imagined than real. On the previous Canadian visit to Moscow, Phil Esposito and his roomie became convinced they had found a "bug" in the center of the floor. They worked on it with a screwdriver, until they heard a tremendous crash in the room below. Esposito had unscrewed the chandelier.

Q: *Although every hockey fan knows the term "hat trick" means three goals in a game by one player, I've never been able to find a sports buff who could explain the derivation of the term. Can you? —Jim Steiner, Torrance, California.*

A: It originated in England in the late 1880s. When a bowler struck the wicket on three successive tries, his manager would award him a new hat. The term was picked up and popularized in soccer, then hockey. Long ago at amateur games in Canada, fans would pass the hat and contribute money and sometimes watches to the hero who had scored three times.

Q: *Is Jim Londos, former world champion wrestler, alive? If not, when and where did he die? Is it true that he was, or is, the world's richest athlete? —James C. Hartwick, Butte.*

A: Jim Londos lives . . . and how. Nearing eighty, still robust, he is enjoying the multimillion-dollar fortune he accumulated over the years through shrewd investments, including buying hotels cheap during the Depression. Londos, who friends say was never very loose with a buck, earned $100,000 a year and more as a wrestling idol in the days when people could keep most of it. Today he lives on his ranch in the Los Angeles area, where he grows avocados. In this country, at least, he was the Golden Greek before Onassis, and may indeed be the wealthiest of all former pro athletes.

Q: *Each time there is a brawl or riot or some kind of misconduct by the fans in a ball park, I think those must be the worst, then some other crowd tops them. Among the pros, which city is considered to have the worst reputation? —Jeff DeFord, Memphis.*

A: For sheer consistency, you can't beat the fans of Philadelphia who, as pitcher Bo Belinsky once said, would boo a funeral. Philly fans are not unsophisticated, as are those who throw pennies and ice onto the court during basketball games, but they have a perverse quality unmatched in other cities. They proudly wear their reputation for being difficult. When Pat Williams, the promotion-minded general manager of the basketball 76ers, introduced a singing pig as one of his half-time acts, the fans booed the performance unmercifully. "What did they expect of a singing pig," said Williams, defending the star, "the Hallelujah Chorus?"

Q: *How and when did Jimmy The Greek become famous?* —*Charles Southwind, Colorado Springs.*

A: Jimmy (Demetrios Synodinos) Snyder first got national publicity in Walter Winchell's column for winning a $200,000 bet on Harry Truman to defeat Thomas Dewey. Snyder had polled 1,200 women at a California supermarket and found that 70 percent would not vote for a man who had a moustache.

Q: *My favorite actor, Telly Savalas, is supposed to make a movie about the gambler Nick The Greek. Is it actually true that he was the biggest bettor of all time? Anything you know about Nick The Greek will be appreciated.* —*C. J. Duren, Baltimore.*

A: Nicholas Dandolos was tall, slender, stylish—a great ladies man. Most of his fame as a high roller came because he looked the part, though he did bet in five figures. Dozens of other gamblers were bigger bettors—including another "The Greek," Jimmy Snyder, in his day. In the last years of his life, pros grew leery of Nick when he tried to set up fixed card games.

Q: *I know that Nick The Greek and Jimmy The Greek were two of the highest bettors that ever put money up. Is there any instance where they bet against each other, and how did it come out?* —*Jake Miranda, Colorado City.*

A: In his book *Jimmy The Greek* for Playboy Press, Jimmy Snyder says the only time he bet head-to-head with the late Nick was in a three-set series of $50,000 freeze-out. The game is over when one guy wins all the money. Jimmy took him two out of three.

Q: *The obituaries of H. L. Hunt mentioned that*

*he bet as much as sixty thousand dollars on a game.
What did he bet on, and how did he bet the money?
—Carl England, Augusta, Georgia.*

A: Billionaire Hunt frequently made astounding bets with bookmakers across the country in the days before everyone's phone was tapped. But his passion was for head-to-head betting, and his most famous series of wagers were versus Jimmy "The Greek" Snyder. Hunt would select three games in the Southwest Conference, giving or taking the national line, and Snyder would select three from the Southeastern Conference—at $50,000 a game. Hunts's other notable session was against oilman Ray Ryan. They played gin rummy at $10 a point during a boat trip from New York to Southhampton. Ryan later said he won $240,000.

Q: *I made a few bets now and then, and I have a question—with all the crowd violence going on, in football and basketball, what happens if a game is called off by officials before it's completed? I mean, what happens if I have a bet going? Are all bets off in that spot? —H. G. L., Passaic, New Jersey.*

A: Presumably, your bookmaker would go along with the rules posted on this subject at all Las Vegas betting shops. If all but the final five minutes have been played, in basketball or football, the game is official.

Q: *Joe Jacob's famous line, "I shoulda stood in bed," came after what fight? —Julius D., Baltimore.*

A: You're going back a long way, but the malaprop wasn't uttered by Max Schmeling's manager after a bout. He had been to the 1935 World Series in Detroit and lost a big bet on the Cubs.

Q: *I am down $6,000 after a season of betting basketball, college and pros. Is there some tip you can give me, from the people who bet really big money,*

that might give me an edge? Next year I'll get even.
—Solly Cohn, Brockton, Massachusetts.

A: There are enough "inside" tips to fill a book, but a basic one that is followed by big bettors, hardly without it occurring to them to do otherwise, is this: always get a price from more than one bookmaker. The more the better. In other words, shop for the points on the side of the line you like.

Q: *You have in the past given tips on pro football and baseball betting "systems," and I have won a few going along with those ideas. Do you know of any proven betting ideas about pro basketball? —King Page, Detroit.*

A: The few successful gamblers, such as the redoubtable Lem Banker of Las Vegas, spend up to eighty hours a week and hundreds of dollars every month on phone calls and newspaper subscriptions to keep abreast of college and pro basketball. The average bettor has no comprehension of the volume of information necessary to have a chance at beating the point spread.

However, here is one easy tip to hang onto until the pro basketball playoffs begin: skip the first game of a series, then bet the loser of the previous game. This is supposed to give you an edge in team motivation and psychology. In 1975 and 1976, it worked 80 percent of the time.

Q: *I want to know if Don Johnson started to bowl with a fingertip ball or with a conventional ball? — David Sudia, Latrobe, Philadelphia.*

A: Johnson, one of bowling's top moneywinners, began with the standard model (which accommodates a grip of two knuckles), but switched to the fingertip (one-knuckle grip) long before he turned pro. The fingertip ball permits greater spin control, but it sure give you funny-looking fingertips.

Q: *Not counting Muhammad Ali, how many heavy-*

weights have retired from boxing while they still held the championship? —*Victor Jahnke, Palm Beach.*

A: Five times in the history of the division, up to the present, the champion retired while still in office. They were: Jim Jeffries, 1905; Jack Johnson, 1913; Gene Tunney, 1930; Joe Louis, 1949, and Rocky Marciano, 1956.

No matter how firm Ali's second retirement—or is it his third?—turns out to be, he qualifies for the list at least once. He was the champion in 1967 when he abdicated, in effect, in the U.S. Marshal's office. The World Boxing Association stripped him of the title when he resisted induction into the Army.

Q: *I noticed that several writers complained after the Ali-Norton fight (in November, 1976) that most judges don't feel a champion should lose the title on a decision, and that's why Ali won. Can you tell me how many times the title changed hands on a decision?* —*Martin Brinkman, Norwalk, Connecticut.*

A: History was clearly on the side of Ali. The last time the heavyweight crown was passed on a decision was forty-one years ago, when James J. Braddock defeated Max Baer. Dating back to 1882, it happened that way only two other times: Jack Sharkey over Max Schmeling and Gene Tunney over Jack Dempsey.

Q: *I saw the Ali–Norton fight on closed circuit and thought Ali had won. However, many people, especially the press, thought Norton won. Can you tell me the count on punches landed, punches missed, etc.? I think Ali hit Norton at least 50 percent more times than he got hit.* —*W. Eugene Mitchell, Houston.*

A: The breakdown you want isn't available, but a postmortem of the fifteenth round, arranged for writers skeptical of the outcome, may shed some light. The reporters and referee Arthur Mercante were invited to a private screening of the film at Gallagher's, a New York pub. Mercante agreed on the condition that the round be divided and analyzed in three separate, one-minute parts.

To the surprise of the writers present, nearly all of whom felt that Norton had been robbed, the slow-motion replay showed that the challenger did not throw a single punch in the first minute, and did not really get aggressive until the last forty-five seconds of the round. If Norton had won the fifteenth, said Mercante, he would have given him the decision. In several rounds, Norton fell back on an old club fighter's tactic —coming on strong in the final seconds in an attempt to sway the judges.

The press has always had a problem viewing Ali objectively.

Q: *Can you tell me if Muhammad Ali ever graduated from high school? Also, what was his religion before he became a Black Muslim?* —*Anne Mazzeri, Detroit.*

A: A D-minus student, Ali's graduation was a sort of split decision over the Louisville school board. He was a Protestant until he announced his conversion, the day after he upset Sonny Liston for the heavy-weight title in 1964.

Q: *Is the Max Baer who played Jethro on the "Beverly Hillbillies" the son of the old heavyweight, or is that just a stage name? I have a bet on this. Also, was the original Max Baer Jewish?* —*Norman Pauley, Dayton.*

A: Jethro is indeed the son of the old fighter, tried the ring briefly himself, quit after a half dozen fights with a mixed record and one broken nose. At thirty-eight, the younger Baer is now producing movies, among them *Ode to Billy Joe.* He was raised a Catholic. His father was not Jewish, but wore a Star of David on his boxing trunks because he thought it would be good box office in New York.

Q: *I would appreciate a summary of the career of boxer Jake La Motta. I understand that only one man ever knocked him down. Who was that man?* —Leo Kerrigan, Philadelphia.

Q: *What was Jake La Motta's record, and how many times did he fight Sugar Ray Robinson?* —Craig Miller, Jerome, Idaho.

A: Apparently, La Motta's other career as a TV actor has revived interest in him as a fighter. La Motta, now fifty-five, was a windmill-style banger who would take two to deliver one. He won the middleweight title in 1949 by kayoing Marcel Cerdan in the tenth. (Cerdan was killed in an airplane crash before a rematch could be held.)

He lost the title a year and a half later when Robinson "stopped" him in the thirteenth. La Motta was still on his feet, but helpless, when the ref halted the fight. La Motta was stopped four times by kayoes, but only during the fourth one, against Danny Nardico, did he hit the deck.

Q: *Is there any way of finding out the smallest crowd ever to see a heavyweight championship fight? I just read that the second Dempsey-Tunney fight drew the biggest gate, over 100,000, outdoors in Chicago, and I am curious to know if there is a record for the smallest.* —Wylie Boggs, St. Paul.

A: How quickly we forget. For all the millions who paid millions to see him work, Muhammad Ali (then Cassius Clay) and Sonny Liston drew the smallest paying crowd ever to watch a heavyweight title fight— 2,434 patrons at Lewiston, Maine, in May of 1965. That was the occasion of the so-called phantom punch that kayoed Liston and pretty much ended his career.

Q: *I know that for a while Philadelphia Flyers' star Barry Ashbee feared he would lose an eye from being hit by the puck in a playoff game. Can you tell me how fast a puck goes?* —Vic Leonard, Philadelphia.

A: As fast as 185 miles per hour, which is the record clocked by Bobby Hull.

Q: *I used to be a wrestling fan, but these big ballet dancers in the ring today turn me off. Am I wrong or weren't the bouts on the level back when Strangler Lewis was champ? —Dr. Simon Leeds, St. Louis.*

A: Ed (Strangler) Lewis, the most enduring wrestler in history, had over 6,000 matches. In his mellow years he put it this way: "We had to give the fans some showmanship. Straight wrestling is the dullest thing in the world. Jim Londos and I agreed to a serious match in Kansas City. It ended up a draw, and half the people had walked out."

Q: *I want to know something about Kareem Abdul-Jabbar's religious and political beliefs. I never hear him speak out about anything. Is he a Black Muslim? —Ben Froehling, Dayton.*

A: Abdul-Jabbar is no unthinking jock, or in his case, superjock. He is a convert to orthodox Moslem belief, the really old-time religion of Islam—which is far different from that of the Black Muslims, an American invention out of Detroit.

The great Lakers' center is not political and believes blacks can help themselves better in other ways: "We need positive, realistic ideas directed at our people. Libraries, education, and hard work. Ninety-seven percent of our people have never had the patience. They want immediate results. One problem is the climate of racism, but another problem is that our people are not willing to work and wait. It is the mentality of laying off blame, of wanting things on a silver platter, the problem of internalized defeat."

Q: *Who is that fellow who appears in the telephone commercial with Bill Russell? They talk like they've been friends a long time. Is Russell's sidekick a former athlete? —Hudson Willse, Butte.*

A: Wake Forest graduate Ronnie Watts spent just enough time in the NBA to complete a long-distance call. He appeared in one game for the Celtics in the 1965-66 season, played in twenty-six games the next, and has already had more TV exposure from the Bell System commercial than in his entire pro career.

Q: *I'm a Hoosier and crazy about basketball. What the pros are playing today is beautiful to watch, but it isn't basketball as I remember it. I remember Cliff Wells and Everett Case coaching high school games that ended 5-4. If I'm not mistaken, even pro games not long ago emphasized ball control and strategy. The suspense in those games was great. Can you tell me how long ago it was the pros played a low-scoring game?* —Craig Wolsterhoos, Hammond, Indiana.

A: On November 22, 1950, the lowest scoring game in NBA history was won by Fort Wayne, 19-18, over a Minneapolis team whose lineup included George Mikan, Slater Martin, Jim Pollard, Vern Mikkelsen, and one Bud Grant, who later played for the Philadelphia Eagles and coached the Minnesota Vikings. Grant was held scoreless. Mikan got 15.

Q: *Pro basketball players are always hinting about a torrid thing Wilt Chamberlain had going with a famous Hollywood star. Is there any truth in it and if so, who was it?* —Annie Howard, San Francisco.

A: The world's tallest playboy, also known as the Big Dipper, a few years ago held a very good and dear friendship with Kim Novak, not normally a sports fan.

Q: *For weeks before the trade was made, everybody seemed to know that Kareem Abdul-Jabbar was going to Los Angeles. Can you explain how something like that gets out? Did Kareem talk?* —Erwin Zabel, Decatur, Illinois.

A: He didn't have to talk. A pretty good clue

emerged at the NBA meetings, when it came time to vote on whether to retain the center jump. The Lakers voted in favor of keeping it, and Milwaukee voted to get rid of it.

Q. *I can't get used to the idea of young athletes turning pro right out of high school. It's a harmful practice, but I fear that the success of Moses Malone will encourage a lot more of it. Can you tell me anything about his background?* —Dr. Elliott Kabaker, St. Louis.

A: Signed by the Utah Stars in 1974, Malone came from what is euphemistically referred to as a deprived background. His father left home when Moses was a child. He did not sleep in a bed of his own until two years before he signed his pro contract. He rarely owned more than one pair of shoes at a time, not including sneakers. Whatever else he was deprived of, basketball wasn't one of them. Near his house in Petersburg, Virginia, was a playground with lights operated by a coin machine. A quarter would buy an hour of time. Malone saved his quarters for the basketball court, playing in games in which the losers would pay for the next hour. If his opponents, or his quarters, held out, Moses would sometimes play all night.

Q: *Wasn't Otto Graham the last player to make All-America in both football and basketball? I'm also betting he's the only one who ever did it.* —Larry Vosmik, Detroit.

A: Technically, Ray Evans of Kansas was the last fellow to pull off the double All-America. He made it in basketball in 1942 and, with time out for war, in football in 1947. Graham earned the honors at Northwestern in 1943-44. The same thing had been done before, but rarely. The select list: Wes Fesler, Ohio State, 1930-31; Benny Oosterbaan, Michigan, 1927-28; Banks McFadden, Clemson, 1939.

Q: *This question may sound foolish but after work-*

ing out a few proportions I have found that the average person can reach up and touch something 1.4 times as high as his height. This involves standing on his toes and stretching up as high as he can with one arm. Applying this to a giant such as Kareem Abdul-Jabbar, at 7 feet, 3 and ⅝ inches, it seems he could touch the rim of a basket without leaving the ground. The question, of course, is can he? —Gary Bertsos, Ann Arbor, Michigan.

A: Yes, he can, but standing flat-footed under the basket is a sure way of getting your toes stepped on. Of more interest to the pros is how high a player can jump from a flat-footed start. Both Kareem and Wilt Chamberlain had a jumping range of 34 inches. By comparison, David Thompson, who may be the greatest leaper the sport has seen, has been taped at 42 inches.

Q: *In a story about the death of Dr. Forrest "Phog" Allen it mentioned that when Wilt Chamberlain announced he was going to Kansas University, the coach said, "I hope he comes out for the team." Has it ever come out what Allen paid Wilt to get him way out in Kansas? —Art Caudle, Philadelphia.*

A: The NCAA investigated a report that a $30,000 slush fund was provided by Kansas businessmen, but Wilt denied it and still does.

"The total was under $20,000," he says. Wilt was given a list of Kansas alums who would keep him solvent. "But I rarely had to ask for money," he says. "We were winning so many basketball games, they'd come up to me in the locker room and stuff $10 bills and $100 bills in my pockets. I never kept any records."

Q: *Is John Havlicek of the Celtics married? —Ona C., Detroit.*

A: John is very much married and you should notice the next time he steps to the free throw line that he brushes his hair back with one hand. This mannerism is a private signal to his pretty bride back in Boston that he's thinking of her.

Q: *I say Kentucky holds the college basketball record for the most winning seasons in a row with 44. My buddy showed me a press clipping that says Louisville owns that record, which is 29. What's the catch here? —Oscar B., Kansas City.*

A: The catch is how you phrase the record. If "consecutive" winning seasons is specified, then Louisville is the champ. Kentucky's string of 44 spans the NCAA suspension that sidelined the Wildcats for the 1952-53 season. Kentucky was swept up in the fix scandals of the early 50s after a defiant Adolph Rupp had claimed, "They couldn't touch my boys with a ten-foot pole." The late Kentucky trainer Smokey Harper said Rupp nearly had apoplexy the day an eleven-foot pole arrived, parcel post, from the Chicago basketball writers.

Q: *You had a note about Moses Malone and his transition from high school ball to the pros. But you didn't say what was the biggest difference between them. Has he said? —Willard Eskew, Austin.*

A: "In pro ball," says Moses, "the people get old. In high school they're all young." Out of the mouths of babes, etc., etc.

Q: *How do you become a professional basketball referee? None of us knows where they come from. —A. Gladman, Mount Vernon, New York.*

A: Mendy Rudolph, chief NBA referee, says you start with pickup games, graduate to high school contests, and on up the ladder. The NBA scouts college refs. Mendy also has a philosophy: "I'm always aware of the crowd, but I never show it. I try to act as if, for all I knew, I was working the game in an empty arena." For detailed advice, you can write NBA's supervisor of officials, John Nucatola, National Basketball Association, 2 Pennsylvania Avenue, New York, New York 10001.

Q: *I think that was sick the way you used Wilt Chamberlain linked with Kim Novak. It also makes me sick the other way. Hasn't anybody told Chamberlain black is beautiful? —Altamease S., Chicago.*

A: Chamberlain has taken a lot of flak for his interracial propensities, but he doesn't back off on the subject. "In my income bracket," he said, "I'm with more white people than I am with black. What am I supposed to do, get into a town and go roaming looking for a black girl? When you're in France you're with French women, in Italy you're with Italian women."

Q: *I know Sammy Davis, Jr., had second thoughts about the big hug he gave Richard Nixon, but I haven't seen anything lately from another great Republican campaigner, Wilt Chamberlain. Has Wilt recanted, too? —Otis Sinclair, Seattle.*

A: Chamberlain was originally a staunch backer of "Richard," as he always called him, but he had a more lukewarm view of the man that other followers. "Looking back on it," Wilt says, "I was subconsciously influenced to back Richard by several things he and I had in common. Throughout his political career, he'd been called a 'loser,' the guy who could never win the big one. Me, too.

"As it turned out, I was deceiving myself about having much input in the White House after Richard was elected. I didn't realize how insulated the President of the United States is after he's elected. Does that mean he exploited me? Sure. . . . After the [1968] convention, I went to see Richard. 'How can I sell Spiro to black people?' I asked him. 'Don't judge Spiro until you've talked to him,' Richard said. . . . Well, I met with Spiro. The next day I told Richard, 'You gonna have some problems with Mr. Spiro.'

"I learned a few lessons the hard way. . . . All the bickering and infighting and maneuvering for access to the candidate wasn't much different than the way people act around athletes and movie stars and other celebrities. When I saw PhD's and other people of that caliber volunteering to wash dishes and run errands, just so they could say they were close to Richard and his top advisors, it reminded me a lot of the starry-eyed groupies and go-fers who hang around sports arenas." Chamberlain didn't campaign for Nixon in 1972.

Q: *Why does Bill Russell always put the blast on Boston? Didn't the Celtics pay him enough when they were winning all those championships? —Art Welch, New Rochelle, New York.*

A: When you see Russell's criticism of "Boston," read "city of," not the Celtics. When Russell quit the Celtics in 1970, he called Boston "the most racist city in the country," but declined to elaborate. Now he is reminding everyone of that opinion and citing the city's school troubles and beach riots.

Q: *Has basketball always kept track of rebounding? If not, when did they start, who was the first college player ever to lead the nation, and how tall was he? —Murray Gargan, Roanoke, Virginia.*

A: The NCAA did not list rebounds as a statistical category until 1951. That year the best board man in the country was Ernie Beck of Penn, who at 6-4 would most likely line up today at guard.

Q: *This may be touchy but I need an answer. What do the pros mean when they say someone plays "black basketball or white basketball"? Can you explain that? Is it a racial putdown? —Norman Niebold, Phoenix.*

A: The term refers to styles, not color, and the origin of it can be traced to playgrounds of the East. No, it isn't discriminatory. It reflects the candor found in few places other than a locker room. A player whose style is "black" can be said to have a liquid grace, an array of moves, and a deadpan ease at making the spectacular play. Think of Julius Erving and Bob Mc-Adoo. But think, too, of Pete Maravich and Rick Berry.

Players who typify the "white" style are intense, mechanical, precise, such as John Havlicek and Rudy Tomjanovich. But Paul Silas and Jim McMillian, both black, are rated by their peers in the "white" category.

Q: *You can have Dr. J. and Kareem. To me, the most colorful player in pro basketball is Slick Watts of Seattle. I don't think he gets the ink he deserves. I'd like any information you can give me about him, but I have two questions in particular. Does the headband he wears serve a purpose, or is it just for effect? Also, I read where Bill Russell once chewed him out during a game. Do they get along?* —*Donnie Plotkin, Atlanta.*

A: Donald (Slick) Watts is the NBA's Cinderella Man. Undrafted in 1973, he wangled a tryout with the Sonics through the efforts of his college coach. "I was lucky," he says, "to come to a team with twelve great shooters and nobody to pass the ball." The headband has become Slick's trademark, but it keeps out of his eyes the perspiration that pours off his balding dome. Probably no player in the league appears before more clubs, gives more talks, or signs more autographs.

Big Bill Russell has a feeling close to love for the bubbly 6 foot 1 inch guard, but does lose patience when Watts—as Russell puts it—"looks into the mirror and sees Walt Frazier." Counters Slick: "Sometimes he tells me my headband is too tight. Sometimes he loses me—I don't understand. But I go sit by the fire and think about it."

Q: *A friend of mine in North Carolina entered a sports trivia contest. The question was: What one athlete played in the NCAA basketball finals, the Rose Bowl and the Super Bowl? He got someone at Sports Illustrated to run it through a computer, and the name that came out was Joe Kapp. Can this be right?* —*Maynard Gimble, Houston.*

A: It is so close to right that SI can be forgiven a minor computer error. Kapp, the U. of California star who led the Bears to the Rose Bowl and later the Vikings to the Super Bowl, was originally recruited as a basketball player. He played his first three years for Cal in that sport, until his football action had made him too muscle-tight to perform well. He was a squadman on the team that reached the second round of the NCAA tournament against Brigham Young. But he did not play when Cal went to the finals in 1959, and won it all.

His coach, Pete Newell, remembers him well: "The spirit that carried that team so far was the spirit infused by Joe Kapp earlier. He was the greatest team-man I ever had. When one of our players was not cheering enough, he'd get up and order the guy to 'go sit on the other bench.' He'd say, 'If you're not going to help us, go help them.' "

Q: *It never ceases to amaze me when the "Wide World of Sports" comes on the air with their "thrill of Victory and the agony of defeat." I have always wondered who the skier is, or was, that took the awful spill. It's difficult to believe that he lived through that fall. —James R. Moore, West Palm Beach.*

Q: *Who is he? From what country? How seriously was he injured? Does he still compete as a jumper? —John Maloney, Helena, Montana.*

Q: *Who is the man crashing over the side of the ski jump; when and where did it happen? —Dave Winston, Houston.*

A: The skier who has come to symbolize ABC's "agony of defeat" is Vienko Bogatej, of Yugoslavia, who escaped with only minor injuries when he took his classic tumble in 1970, during the international ski flying championships at Obersdorf, West Germany. Bogatej was back competing within a matter of weeks. One of the top European skiers at the time, he gained far more exposure by failing, thanks to ABC's alert camera work, than he ever did by winning.

Q: *It's not clear to me what assurances the Russians*

gave the Olympic committee about protecting the individual rights of fans attending the 1980 Games in Moscow. The whole question seems impossible to me. —Dennis Martendale, Anderson, Indiana.

A: In the next several years it is hoped these assurances will be nailed down, based on the experiences of Team Canada visits. Bob Woolf, the Boston sports attorney who was in the official party on one of those trips, tells a hairy story of what happened to a Canadian fan who insisted on blowing a bugle in the stands.

After he ignored several *"Nyets"* from the Russian guards, he was jailed on a charge of drunkenness, had his head shaved, and was placed under a cold shower for eight hours. His prison number was tattooed on his heels. He was fined $260 and sentenced to one-to-three years in jail, beginning with fifteen days at hard labor. The Canadian ambassador finally secured his release.

The fear in the sports world is that the Russians do not really comprehend the playful havoc that comes with an Olympic Games crowd.

Q: *What's the most often asked question in sports? —David F., Seattle.*

A: You've just asked it. The runner-up is the one about who succeeded Gene Tunney as heavyweight champ, with all the confusion from there until the time Joe Louis took over. One more time: Tunney retired. Schmeling won the vacated title on a foul by Sharkey. Sharkey then beat Schmeling. Carnera "kayoed" Sharkey. Baer really knocked out Carnera. Braddock decisioned Baer. And Louis kayoed Braddock. Got it?

SPRING

"There are two things a man can enjoy without being good at," Jimmy Demaret once confided, "golf and sex." There is a humor, an attitude, a social quality at work on the fairways that exists in no other sport—well, no other outdoor sport. No one ever captured that feeling more fully than Demaret, whose influence on the game spans the past forty-odd years. He was golf's original bon vivant, a fashion plate, the man most credited with lifting the sport out of the knickers-and-necktie era. As a player and later a television analyst—and three times a Masters champion—Demaret has seen it all, dating back to the days when a professional entered a country club through the kitchen. Today he owns one, with Jack Burke, Jr., the prestigious Champions Golf Club, in Houston.

Jimmy Demaret:
The Golfer

QUESTION: To begin with, many of today's pro golfers emerge from the college ranks. From what training ground did a Jimmy Demaret come?

JIMMY DEMARET: From the caddie shop. Going back to when I first got started, which is about 1917, right at the end of World War I, your big names in golf were mostly English, fellows like Harry Vardon and Ted Ray, and here in America we had the Walter Hagens and the Gene Sarazens, and they all came out of the caddie ranks. And now the kilowatt has replaced the caddie. You know, the electric golf cart.

Q.: At a time when there was very little money in golf, what persuaded you to attempt it as a career?

J.D.: Actually, I was a victim of circumstances. I was playing sandlot baseball around Camp Logan, a military base near Houston, and one day this major came over and asked if I wanted to caddie. I kind of liked it, and I caddied until I was about sixteen, and then I started as an assistant pro. To tell the truth, I don't know why I kept at it, because in those days I used to take my clubs to the ball field and I was considered sort of a sissy or something. In those days 99 percent of the kids didn't know what the hell golf was.

Q.: When you finally took a shot at the pro tour, how did you finance yourself?

J.D.: Well, I was an assistant pro at Galveston, and I used to give lessons to the late Ben Bernie, who was an orchestra leader in those days. In 1934, I think it was, I won the Texas PGA in Dallas, and so Ben and two other Galveston men offered to back me on the tour. They gave me $500 and, you know, in those days that was a pretty good amount. So we headed for California, three of us in an old Model-T Ford. We were in El Paso and we had a few dollars and a siphon for gasoline. We weren't above stealing a few gallons of gas, I must admit. And we had a few cans of pork 'n' beans, and we were looking for ways to pick up a little money along the way. These friends I was with, one of them said he was quite a pool player, and so we stopped off in Juarez, and the first night we blew everything we had. We caddied a few days to build up another pile, and then we went back and lost that. The next thing you know we lost the car and we had to hock my golf clubs. We took a freight train out west and I wired my brother Milton for money to get my clubs out of hock, and that was the start of my first tour.

Q.: With a beginning like that, you had to sink at least a forty-foot uphill putt to win your very first tournament.

J.D.: Nope. Finished third. Walter Hagen shot a 66 in the last round to beat me out of second place. Jug McSpaden won it. This was at Sacramento. I took my share of the prize money and threw a party.

Q.: You never really became a part of the constant tour-scene. Why was that?

J.D.: I was never a free-lancer, like most of today's pros. I've always been connected with a club, and I think the most tournaments I ever played in one year was fourteen. Some of these fellows play forty or fifty a year. I always felt that I owed my club more time than I owed my tour.

Q.: But suppose you had come along in today's inflated market. Wouldn't you have been tempted to teach less and play more?

J.D.: Well, I don't know. I think today there are two different breeds entirely, pro golfers who play on the tour, and golf professionals who stay at home and play in only a few tournaments. I don't consider as true professionals those who have never had any experience in, say, building a set of clubs from scratch, or shining clubs or wrapping them.

Q.: Are young prospects likely to be spoiled by the big purses, the endorsement money and sponsorship?

J.D.: Let's just say that they don't really know what the hell it is to struggle. I was talking to a golfer the other day who had never worked at anything in his life. He says to me, "You know, I have a sponsor now." I'm stunned. I say, "Great, that's wonderful, but it's a little expensive to operate if you're thinking of trying the tour." He says, "Well, they're giving me $15,000 a year plus per diem." All I could say was, "My gosh, man, I was the leading money winner in 1947. I won six tournaments, finished second seven times—and won $24,000."

Q.: Jimmy, you came along and with your flamboyant ways and your colorful manner of dress, you added another dimension to the game. Now, was this in any way a calculated plan of yours?

J.D.: No, I certainly didn't calculate. I remember my father was a painter and I used to mix paint with him in the barn, and he'd slap two or three paints together and come out with another color. And, of course, when I was a kid, a man's old blue serge, worn-out, slick-assed pants, you know, was his golf attire. He screwed a few spikes in his half sole shoes, and this was golf attire, and an old stinky sweater and a stinky shirt. But when I kept playing and I saw these lovely colors that the ladies wore around, I'd travel to New York and go to a tailor and I couldn't afford the tailor, but I'd say, "How can I get some of these colors?" And he said, "Geez, you must be kidding." And he said, "Well, I'll have to order them from the ladies' materials out of England." And I said, "Well, order them. I want slacks this way and coats this way." And I used to get whistled at, you know, in the gallery. Lavender slacks and chartreuse coats, and I'd take the fabric and send it up to Boston and have the fabric sewn into the saddle on the shoes, and this was back in '38, '39, and they thought I was a flat idiot.

Q.: Well, how could you afford it?

J.D.: I afforded it by putting my money that I won into these things, because this was what I liked. I couldn't afford it, really.

Q.: But in a way it sort of came back to you. It helped to make Jimmy Demaret better known and it set you apart from the run-of-the-mill golfers. People associate Demaret with bringing a quality of show business to the sport. If you hadn't gone into golf as a career, would you have tried the entertainment arts?

J.D.: I imagine I would have. I remember years ago, about 1936, I was in California, and I was at the Hillcrest Golf Club, and a William Morris agent came out and visited the club. Al Jolson was living at that time, he was singing there, and Eddie Cantor and Georgie Jessel and all of them, and they had this party and I got up and sang, strictly . . . you know, amateurish, and this fellow with the William Morris Agency, he says, "Hey," he said, "Jimmy, could we book you at the Paramount Theatre in New York as a singing golfer?" And I said, "Geez, I'm on the tour. I like golf. I don't want to be a singer." He said, "We'll give you $1,500 a week." Well, I wasn't making any $1,500 a week. So there was a decision there whether I should go to Paramount and make an ass out of myself, jumping up and singing, or stay on the tour, and I felt, well, my chances are a little better on the tour.

Q.: Didn't you at one time sing with Ben Bernie?

J.D.: Yeah, I sang with Ben Bernie. I sang with Lawrence Welk, and I never shall forget one time I was playing in the Open, in 1940, in Cleveland. And they had a little orchestra there led by Sammy Watkins at one of the hotels. And they had a singer sitting on the bench with a big nose, and his name was Dean Martin. And so Sammy used to get me to sing, because I was the star at the golf tournament, and so Dean was sitting on the front stool there. He was the singer with them. And Dean always accused me of trying to beat him out of his job with Sammy Watkins. Every time I see him he says, "You son of a bitch. Remember you tried to beat me out of a job?"

Q.: I don't guess really that there's ever been a golfer more popular than you with the people in the sport, and people in the performing arts, and just the fans who have followed it. Have you ever met a golfer you didn't like?

J.D.: No. No, I really haven't. I'll be honest with you. I've met some that, you know, I might go on the back nine when they're teeing off on the first nine, but I don't think I've ever met anyone that I didn't like. We may have different ideas about golf, but . . . no, I don't think so. I think golf is the strangest game in the world. I think it brings out the truth in a man more than any sport I've ever seen. You can walk around with some fellow and you can really understand him after you've played eighteen holes with him. You know what kind of businessman he is, what kind of doctor he is, or what kind of a sport he is, just by playing eighteen holes of golf with him. Damn, it'll come out in him, you know?

Q.: If there was one mythical major tournament, and in it you could enter every golfer of your experience, in their prime, who do you think would win?

J.D.: Oh, I think Ben Hogan easy. I think Ben had every shot in the bag. He was a magnificent concentrator. He was the kind of guy who could isolate himself from everything but knocking the ball in the cup, and of all the great players I've ever seen and played with and watched and have admiration for, I would say Ben Hogan is the greatest golfer. I would say that Arnold Palmer probably, in my time, going back to Walter Hagen, even, or Bobby Jones or anyone else, I think Arnold Palmer is the most radiant personality I guess the game has ever known. You could stick competitors in there like Sarazen, Hagen. They were great competitors. But I think the greatest golfer that I've ever seen in my life, tee to green and through the green, anywhere you put him he had the shot for the situation,

103

would be Ben Hogan. He was great under the worst kind of pressure.

Q.: Although you were such opposite types, many people assume that you've been close to Hogan, closer than anyone. How do you account for it?

J.D.: Well, we aren't close. The strangest thing in the world is that Ben and I have never been close. I don't know Ben. We played together in competition, but, actually, on the tour Ben and I never ran together. I have all the admiration for Ben Hogan, but we had never actually been that close, because nobody gets close to Ben Hogan.

Q.: Well, do you have any favorite Hogan stories that sort of illustrate the unique personality of the man?

J.D.: One time we were playing in a tournament in Rochester, New York, many years ago, and it was the Oak Hill Golf Club, where Trevino won the Open. And we went out and played and Ben Hogan shot a 64 with a double bogey on number seventeen, which is a long four par. He made a six on it, and this is a hell of a round, you know. We were all playing in the tournament, so Lloyd Mangrum and Craig Wood and myself, we were playing gin rummy after we came in the clubhouse, and having a few drinks, and as I was driving out right before dark, I see this fellow practicing out there, and I saw he had a few people around him, and it looked like Ben. So I stopped the car, and I said, "For Pete's sake, Ben," I said, "you've been out here practicing since you came in?" He said, "Yeah." I said, "Well, Ben, you had about ten birdies or something like that, shot 64 with a double bogey. What the hell are you trying to prove?" He says, "Jimmy, there's no reason in the world why a man can't birdie every hole."

Q.: Of your many accomplishments in golf, which do you cherish the most? Which title or honor or distinction?

J.D.: Well, I would say the most pleasure I ever got out of golf, I guess, was with people that I met in the game. I'd say that the biggest pleasure as a competitor would be winning the Masters, being the first three-time Masters champion. I would say, after analyzing the Augusta National Golf Club, I don't know how I ever won the Masters Tournament, really. Because all of my life I've faded the ball and it's sort of a hooker's golf course, and I've been a fader all of my life. But I've tried to figure this thing out and I don't know how in the hell I ever won it, except that I . . . I like the beauty of the place, I like the surroundings, I like the challenge, and I seemed to be able to hold my composure more when I had a chance to win. When I was just a few shots back, I was lackadaisical. I didn't give a damn. But when I had a chance to win, I always felt I could go forward, and I think this had more to do with it than anything. I liked the way the tournament was run. It is the epitome of the operation of a golf event, like the Kentucky Derby or the Indianapolis 500 or the World Series or the Super Bowl.

Q.: Some people claim that golfers are not athletes in the truest sense. How do you answer that theory?

J.D.: Well, that's the silliest statement I've ever heard in my life. When I see a football player in for two or three downs, and then he goes and sits on the bench and gets oxygen . . . I see baseball players who are the greatest in the world, like your Musials and your Williamses and your Babe Ruths. These guys stand out there all day and never catch a fly, never move, you know. And I see a golfer out there for six hours at a time, with a tremendous strain . . . mentally, on his nervous system. The first thing that goes with a golfer is his nervous condition. When his nerves are gone, he's had it. I think golfers are the greatest athletes in the world, myself.

Q.: The age of Palmer is coming to an end now. Do you think that golf will continue to produce the super hero, or is it reaching a point where a different guy is going to win every week?

J.D.: I think right now you're going to find different fellows winning tournaments, and I hate to see it, for the simple reason that I think any sport needs a leader.

Baseball right now is in a period of decay to me. I could care less. And I love all sports. But now they don't have leaders. They don't have a fellow that the world follows. They don't have a Babe Ruth or a Ted Williams. They just don't have them. They try to build them up but they flop. But in golf, the man builds himself up. Nobody else . . . his teammates are not going to build him up. And I just hope when Palmer and Nicklaus leave the scene that some guy will sneak in and . . . I don't see it in the seventies, I really don't. I do not see it in the seventies. I hope it's just a transition period.

Q.: A last question and an obvious one. What do you tell the young golfers who come to you for advice, who want to turn pro, who read about those big jackpots and endorsements?

J.D.: Well, I've found out in the years of my life that it's difficult to give advice. Actually I am glad to see a boy who has any chance at all get out and find out for himself. I'm not going to tell him he can't make it, even if I know in my heart that he can't. But I say, "Well, you'll never know until you try it one time. It's a rough business and you'll find out for yourself." If I tell him anything else, he wouldn't pay any attention anyway. So I took my own advice once. I just went out and tried it myself, and I wish more boys would do that right now, instead of falling back on their sponsors. My friends told me, "Wire me if you need anything." Fortunately, that telegram never got sent. You know, if I had ever wired them for money, I'd never have been worth a damned thing.

Questions & Answers

Q: *I was watching a golf tournament on TV, one of those won by Johnny Miller, and I heard them credit*

Arnold Palmer with the rise of golf into a multimillion-dollar tour. It seems to me that television is responsible and Palmer is just the guy the public focused on. Isn't the rise of TV the reason golf boomed? —Arthur Lowell, Salt Lake City.

A: Sports historians generally credit the boom to three factors—Arnie's charisma, television's attention, and the presence of a golfer in the White House. Dwight Eisenhower had a putting green installed on the White House lawn, lived as often as he could in Augusta, and delighted in a dollar Nassau versus various pros, including Arnie. Ike's escape to the links was a papal blessing for any businessman who wanted to follow.

Q: *Among the top pro golfers, can you tell me which one is considered the fastest player?* —Eleanor Dodge, St. Louis.

A: Probably Lee Trevino, who says, "I've always played fast. My ambition is to play behind myself."

Q: *Can you tell me if it's true that match play has all but gone from gold because of the dangers of a fix? A tournament can't be "thrown," but a head-to-head match can.* —Tucker Karp, Fort Lauderdale.

A: Professional golf dropped match play as an occasional format because it too often resulted in finals that featured a nobody. However, you are correct in that rumors of a fix were often rampant at such events. In the early years of the Tournament of Champions, when match play was still in vogue, the word was once spread that co-favorite Doug Ford was "in the tank" to Arnold Palmer. The rumor was squelched, and all suspicion removed, when a Las Vegas gambler spotted Ford in a Catholic church the morning of the match, on his knees, praying. "Nobody," concluded the gambler, "is going to throw a match an hour and a half after he leaves church."

STRICTLY PERSONAL: To Lorraine M., Boca

Raton, Florida.—The answer to your question about the ladies pro golf tour is yes, but the subject is libelous.

Q: *I caught Buddy Hackett's act at Lake Tahoe and he went on and on about Jimmy Demaret, the old golfer, and how he taught him to play the game. Some of it was funny, but how much was true? —Shepherd Marx, Omaha.*

A: Demaret, three times Masters champion, is noted as a raconteur. He did, indeed, give Hackett (whom Demaret calls Buddy Hacker) a few lessons while he was the pro in the Catskills. Hackett said he once asked Demaret if golf was better than booze and broads, and Jimmy replied, "Young fella, I have been playing golf thirty years so I could afford booze and broads."

Q: *A few years ago I found an old golf club which has a wooden handle, with Harry Vardon's name on it. Could you please tell me who Harry Vardon was and what years did he play the sport? Also, could you give me some info about the club—it is a "72" putter. —Charles Lunsted, Stanwood, Michigan.*

A: Harry Vardon, the Bobby Jones of England, won the British Open six times between 1896 and 1914, and won the U. S. Open in 1900. It was the excitement of Francis Ouimet's victory over Vardon and fellow Briton Ted Ray, in a playoff for the 1913 U. S. Open, that boomed golf into a national sport here.

The "72" putter was so named because 72 was a sensational golf score in Vardon's day. His fame is immortalized in today's PGA Vardon Trophy, which goes to the pro with the lowest per-round average for the year.

Q: *Nightclub singer Don Cherry gets a lot of publicity out of being a championship golfer. What pro-am did he play in? —Harv Stallings, San Diego.*

A: Cherry wasn't as great a golfer as his publicity man thinks he was, but he did establish a record for low amateur score in the U. S. Open with a 284. The mark was shared with another amateur in that 1960 field, Jack Nicklaus.

Q: *I have been hearing some disturbing things about a great hero of mine [name withheld]. I wouldn't put any belief in it, except he has been going so bad on the pro tour. Do you know if [deleted] is having some off-course problems? —Danny Whiting, Miami.*

A: Your question turned up a surprising and unhappy bit of scandal. The man you named, a great golfer in his time, has been bankrolling a private blackjack game run by a girlfriend of his in a city far from his hometown. His friends are desperately trying to dissuade him from this pastime, but his passion for the dealer is such that he won't listen. We hope this never hits a police blotter, because it would disillusion most of the country's sports fans.

Q: *The stories about Ed Sullivan's death said he started out as a sportswriter. I go way back and I only remember Sullivan as a Broadway columnist. What did he ever do as a sportswriter? —Kenny Coughlin, Dayton.*

A: Sullivan never forgot that a unique sports event —and his charming story—got him back into the newspaper business when he was on his uppers. Grantland Rice had gotten him a job as golf secretary at a resort hotel in Ormond Beach, Florida. In 1922, he filed a story for the wire services about a golf match between John D. Rockefeller and railroad magnate George D. Baker. The yarn drew a job offer from the *New York Graphic* and Sullivan was back in the big time to stay.

Q: *If Tom Weiskopf walks out of a golf tournament in a fit of anger, does the PGA or anybody else in golf take any action? Can he just keep doing this? —Walter Englehardt, Fort Wayne.*

A: Weiskopf, a talented and otherwise likable fellow

109

who is cursed by self-indulgence, has walked out of four tournaments in one year and was fined a total of $3,000 by golf commissioner Deane Beman. Beman also put Weiskopf on a year's probation, under threat of suspension. Weiskopf had said the death of his father matured him, but you can't change lifelong personal traits overnight.

Q: *The women's Superstars Show on TV gave me a laugh. I had to wonder what my greatest all-time gal would have done in that company. I mean Babe Didrikson, who was as great as the other Babe in her own way. If she came along today, what sport would she compete in? —Uhlie Bengston, Madison.*

A: Mildred Didrikson won two individual gold medals in the 1932 Olympics (hurdles, javelin) and never found a sport she couldn't master. She once pitched three innings against the St. Louis Cardinals in an exhibition game, and allowed one run. The Babe was, and is, the greatest women's golfer of all time, but if she were around today she would take one look at the tennis prizes, then proceed to win Wimbledon, Forest Hills, and whatever else they wanted to put up. She died at age forty-two, winning the U. S. Open between operations for cancer.

The Babe was also a champion off the playing field. Her friends recall the twilight evenings at a golf course when she and buddy Betty Dodd (on the guitar) would have a singsong with Louise Suggs and Patty Berg, rendering "San Antonio Rose" and "You Are My Sunshine." The girls could sing, and live, in harmony.

Q: *How large was Babe Didrikson? —Ida Lake, Pinehurst, North Carolina.*

A: In her prime, Mildred Ella Didrikson was 5 feet 6½ inches and weighed 130 pounds, with gusts up to 170 in her later years as a golf pro. Her friend and golfing rival, Betty Hicks, describes the early Babe as "bosomless and narrow-thin with hacked-off hair." Her language was graphic.

Q: *Why don't the pro golfers in their TV tournaments line up their putts simultaneously before putting? This would speed play tremendously over the individual alignments.* —B. B. Burroughs, Cincinnati.

A: With a threesome, this could lead to mass confusion, much stepping in the line of the other guy's putt, and maybe a few accidental knockdowns. Most of all, it would be too distracting to the players. Putts, remember, make up half of a par score.

The worst result of this is how it slows play among everyday hackers, who imitate the procedures of their TV heroes. "Most amateurs," says Lee Trevino, "look at a putt five ways and don't know what they're looking for."

Q: *Sam Snead holds the record for most tournament wins. At today's prices, how much would old Sam's wins be worth?* —Gus L., New Orleans.

A: $1,865,746.10.

Q: *Who was the latest amateur to win a PGA tournament?* —Zeke M., Portland, Maine.

A: Doug Sanders was an amateur when he won the 1956 Canadian Open. No one has done it since.

Q: *As far as I know, what nobody noticed about Jack Nicklaus the last day of the Masters was the one tip-off on how confident he was he would win—he wore a green sport shirt so it would match the green coat he got at the end of the final round. Did anyone ever ask him about his selection of clothes?* —Daniel Crane, Knoxville.

A: Reporter Lee Winfrey told us something about this we never knew until now: "My clothes are determined by my TV commercials scheduled for that day," says Nicklaus. "When they're being advertised, I'm supposed to wear them. I'm told what shirts and slacks to wear every Saturday and Sunday because those are the TV days."

Q: *Ben Hogan has just been voted the big Bobby Jones Award, which I take it is sort of a Hall of Fame. I was trying to tell a friend about Hogan's bus accident and his comeback, etc. But I have forgotten the sequence of events. Didn't Hogan always play with pain after the accident? —Coley Hamilton, Palm Beach.*

A: Hogan had won his first U. S. Open in 1948, before being shattered by a head-on collision with a bus. He later won three more Opens, playing all the way with pain. "I took the attitude," he says now, "that golf was my business and that pain shouldn't bother anybody. Everyone has a little of it. You get used to it. The trouble was, the farther I went on a golf course, the heavier my legs got. I wore a bandage that went from my feet up to my crotch. But you can't feel sorry for yourself."

Q: *My wife and I are arguing about our daughter who wants to run track. I don't care what the women libbers say, I'm against it. Isn't it a fact that competing in sports roughs a girl up? —Ansel King, Las Cruces, New Mexico.*

A: Advocates of women in sports refer to a study by Dr. Christine Pickard, of London, on the subject that is probably bugging you. Said Dr. Pickard: "Athletes are physical creatures. Their bodies are important to them—the physical sensations, touch, the ripple of muscles. Women athletes are more interested in sex and physically more responsive than their less-active sisters." In other words, competing in sports is likely to make your daughter more feminine, not less.

Q: *Is jockey Mary Bacon still a feminine person despite the life she's had to lead on the race track? I mean, she broke up with her husband and does that tell us anything? —Corinne Vaughn, Gary.*

A: Pert and pretty Mary Bacon, who popped topless out of birthday cakes in an earlier career, stays very feminine while earning $75,000 a year booting home winners. She applies three kinds of face cream nightly, uses pink polish on her fingernails and toe-nails, and wears flower-print bikini undies.

"You can see my pants right through my white rac-ing silks," says Mary. "Sometimes the pants have a daisy pattern, sometimes roses. I call it 'flower power.' When the other jocks needle me about it, I just tell them it will give them something to look at when they follow me across the finish line."

Q: *As a Knicks fan I was disappointed that Wilt Chamberlain refused their offer to come out of retire-ment. I read his biography, in which he bragged about his bedroom exploits. Now I see where he spends a lot of his time coaching various women's teams. I can't figure him out. Is that his way of forming a harem, or what?* —*Stan Latham, Newark.*

A: In a departure from his public image, Wilt took up coed sports as a cause in early 1976. He coached a girls' volleyball team, Wilt's Little Dippers, sponsored a track team, Wilt's Wonder Women, and purchased a pro volleyball franchise, the Southern California Rangers. Parents of some of the girls, skeptical at first, grew convinced of his sincerity.

Part of Wilt's motivation had to do with the aborted career of his sister, Barbara, a fine athlete, who in their childhood, found no outlet for her talents in track and basketball. He also believes there is less bigotry in women's sports. Finally, he says: "Partly it's my male instinct. It can be a turn-on to watch beautiful women in action. The most beautiful girls I've ever seen . . . have been on the athletic field."

STRICTLY PERSONAL: To Tommy Kirkland, Black Mountain, North Carolina—Burt Reynolds never played pro football, just a couple of seasons at Florida State. Russia won the most medals. Muhammad Ali is unquestionably the most famous boxer in the history of the sport. Largest fish ever caught on a rod was a 2,664-pound great white shark, by Alf Dean, of Aus-tralia, in 1959. Another 4,500-pound shark was landed by harpoon off Long Island in 1964. Largest of all landed by hand harpoon was a 97-foot whale in 1910.

Q: *Every tennis fan in the world must have figured "Miss World," Marjorie Wallace, would destroy Jimmy Connors before moving on to another sports celebrity, especially when he blew out of Wimbledon in the [1976] quarterfinals. But Jimmy came back to win the U. S. Open, so he must be able to cope with the company. Can you tell me anything about their life-style— or his schedule of training? —Ellen Flannery, Philadelphia.*

A: Miss Wallace is twenty-two, Connors twenty-four, and that has to explain how the world's Number 1 player keeps it going on junk food and his new roommate. Also, as she confides (for public consumption), they often go to bed as early as 8:30 P.M. before a big match, solely to watch TV: "When I say Jimmy is disciplined, I mean disciplined."

Q: *A close friend of mine saw Bill Cosby play a celebrity doubles match and says he kept up a running line of chatter about the game that was hilarious. Does Cosby have any tennis material in his comedy routines? If so, I would like to know how it goes. —Danny Franklin, Baltimore.*

A: Here is Cosby with a tennis tip: "All the greatest pros, during a match, say one thing to themselves over and over again: 'Watch the ball.' That phrase, 'Watch the ball,' is usually followed by the word 'dummy.' Rather than be a dummy, watch the ball. It is also possible to hit the ball too late. When that happens, you hear the pros say, 'Hit the ball in front, dummy.' Of course, you don't have to watch the ball all of the time. If it has gone past you, you don't have to watch it anymore. Also you don't have to call yourself a dummy. Your partner will do it for you."

Q: *I have always admired Arthur Ashe, both for his skill on the tennis court and the way he handles him-*

114

self. He is a gentleman but he is not afraid to speak out. Yet I find that some of my black friends—I am white—are less enthused than I am. Does this reflect a general black attitude toward Arthur? If so, why, and how does he react to it? —Janice Alexander, Sacramento.

A: This is a battle Ashe knows he cannot win. "I play the sport of the country club set," he says, "and a lot of blacks just have no idea what it's all about. But some of my acceptance by whites has to do with physical appearance. That is, if I were real tall, real black, and wore one of those knit hats the brothers wear with the bells hanging down and some clothes that Frenchie Fuqua would wear, with a cape or something, they might not feel the same way . . . [But] when I'm playing on television and it appears that I never get mad, that's not for their sake. That's just the way I was taught to play."

Q: *I have a perplexing question I hope you can answer. My daughter is just starting to play tennis and like all the kids these days she has to use two hands on the backhand. But on the serve this causes a problem because if the first serve doesn't go in, she has to walk to the backstop and get another ball for the second serve. I realize that at tournaments they have ballboys and ballgirls to throw the server another ball, but what do ordinary weekend doublehanders do? —Emily Threlkeld, Little Rock.*

A: Chris Evert popularized the two-handed hit. During her first days on the Virginia Slims circuit, when Ms. Evert's first serve went in, she would toss the extra ball backward as she moved to play the return. This was distracting to her opponent, so now Chrissie holds one at a time, and when the first serve is a fault, she has the extra ball tossed to her by a court attendant.

Now, for average female-type tennis persons, who don't want their costumes cluttered with pockets, there is a new solution. You know the matching undergarment? Well, its elastic is supposed to be just elastic enough to accommodate the second Spalding.

Q: *Bjorn Borg is supposed to be the glamour boy of pro tennis with all the teeny-boppers crowding around him. How does Bjorn handle this? How does he have the strength to play tennis?* —*Kathy G., Gainesville, Florida.*

A: The nineteen-year-old Bjorn (which means "Bear" in Swedish) handles it very well. We asked him about this at a tournament in Dallas and he shrugged, "What would you do? Either they come to the hotel or I meet them somewhere." Borg has a steady girlfriend, Swedish tennis player Helen Anliot, but says he does not intend to get married "for a long time."

Q: *I know that Billie Jean King and her husband Larry are on the outs, but not divorced. Does she have a boyfriend? Are there male groupies on the women's tennis tour?* —*Dody Mathews, Miami.*

A: Billie Jean and Larry have agreed to remain friends and business partners and create their own private lives. Billie Jean, supremely confident on the court, has less confidence in herself as a female and is content to make the tour with her private secretary and traveling companion, Marilyn Barnett. Yes, there is a coterie of male admirers who seem to make the most of the stops on the women's schedule.

Q: *Can you answer once and for all if Billie Jean King swings from both sides of the court? Comprenez?* —*Helen T., Detroit.*

A: We dig. Billie Jean has answered the question once and for all, but not everyone is going to like her reply: "No, I'm not a lesbian. That's not even in the ball park for me. But even though that scene isn't in my bag, I think people should be free to do whatever they want to do and get their pleasure any way they can as long as it doesn't hurt anybody else. I'm for liberation at all levels, be it gay liberation or whatever."

116

Q: *I thought the Bobby Riggs bubble had burst when he got beat by Billie Jean King, but I still see him on TV commercials advertising shaving lotion. Is he just going to go on and on with his gig?* —*Helen W., Denver.*

A: The bubble has poofed. The lotion commercials have been discontinued. But Riggs salvaged a juicy future with one of his last stunts, presenting Billie Jean with a giant Sugar Daddy sucker just before their match. ABC-TV got a great shot of the brand name, and the PR man responsible was so pleased he got Riggs a $100,000 annual contract as club pro for the Tropicana Hotel in Las Vegas.

Q: *Bobby Riggs has a reputation as one of the world's great "hustlers." Do you know the single biggest score Riggs ever put over?* —*Lawrence M., Newport Beach, California.*

A: Legend has it—and Riggs encourages the story—that his biggest "killing" came during World War II when he and Don Budge were both in the service and played a series of matches in the Marianas Islands. Riggs took Budge for all his pro tour savings. Riggs was a petty officer third class whose drinks were served by admirals. Riggs profited two ways from the Marianas matches, inducing tennis king Budge to accept him as a challenger in the first postwar pro tour. Riggs beat Budge throughout that tour . . . and then along came Jack Kramer.

Q: *The pro at my tennis club, who knows a lot of the people involved, says that many of the girls on the Virginia Slims tour aren't speaking these days to Julie Heldman. She is supposed to have embarrassed them by divulging "locker room secrets" in an interview. Do you know anything about this?* —*Helen Ringgold, Fort Lauderdale.*

A: Miss Heldman, an appealing and uninhibited source for reporters, may not have realized how her remarks would look in print. In comparing life on the road with the life-styles of male athletes, Julie told

117

Roger Kahn of *Esquire*: "The women vary. You hear about lesbianism and there is some." After mentioning "two famous names," she went on: "I'd say one is truly lesbian. The other is really asexual. Making money is her sex." On the heterosexual side, Julie told of one woman's reaction to losing a tough match: She announced to a crowded locker room that that night she intended to have romance. "I don't know where," she said. "I don't know by whom." But romance was definitely on her menu.

Q: *I have been watching tennis on television and it seems to me that the crowds have gotten noisier. They root for favorites and applaud errors, and this used to be a gentle, polite game. The players don't seem to complain much, but what do they think of it privately?* —Ken Gagnard, Chicago.

A: Most pros get angry when people applaud a double fault, but the majority approve of the new atmosphere, particularly the lady pros. Says Julie Heldman: "If I don't get applause, I go to pieces. I'm the original Jewish ham. I played in England and beat three sixteen-year-olds in a row. Didn't hear a sound of applause in three days. You know, dirty, nasty Julie Heldman was beating those sweet little things. One match my opponent hit a good shot and got applause. I hit a winner and nothing. So I bowed. After the match, a guy asked me if I was trying to be the Jimmy Connors of women's tennis. I gave him the finger."

Q: *The Boston Lobsters of World Team Tennis are supposed to have a policy of coed showers and locker rooms. Is this on the level? Isn't that carrying togetherness a bit far? If it's not a gag or a publicity stunt, where do I go to sign up?* —Jeff Epstein, Denver.

A: It didn't exactly start out as a team policy, said a spokesman for the Lobs. But separate facilities were not always available and, besides, after four hours of hot, sweaty competition, a tennis clubhouse isn't a very romantic place. "Athletes," added Ron Tiriac, then

Boston's player-coach, "aren't sex maniacs." Most team members considered the unisex showers a healthy trend, proof of which was that Boston teammates Ras Reid and Kerry Melville were married in April, 1975. For a tryout, consult the WTT franchise nearest you.

Q: *Most of the stories about Bjorn Borg refer to him as "emotionless." I find that remarkable in a young man who just turned twenty and has won the U. S. Pro Tennis championship for the third straight year. Is that just part of his character, or a style he developed on the court? He doesn't strike me as a cold fish. —Dr. Paul Lindley, Detroit.*

A: An interesting physical characteristic may account in part for Borg's low-strung disposition, as well as his endurance. The former Teen Angel has a pulse rate in the low 40s, which compares to that of a long-distance runner in track (that was supposedly the secret of Paavo Nurmi, the great Finnish miler, who registered a flat 40 beats per minute).

Arthur Ashe, acknowledging Borg's skill at wearing down his foes, says there is only one way to play him: "Down the middle. You have to keep him from running you all over the court."

Q: *Here we go again. I see where Bruce Jenner, the decathlon champion, is being touted as a possible movie Tarzan. I wonder if you can list all the former athletes who have played Tarzan? —Edward Fitzer, Raleigh, North Carolina.*

A: If they ever held a Tarzan reunion, it would look like an all-sports banquet. The roster would include at least one ex-football player (Mike Henry, L.A. Rams); two swimmers (Buster Crabbe and Johnnie Weismuller); and a track man (Glenn Morris, the 1936 decathlon champ). Don Bragg, the Villanova pole vaulter, earned the nickname—he was known to his friends and public as "Tarzan"—and wanted the part, but never got it.

Q: *I know that Kentucky Derby winners are in demand for stud service. But can you tell me if a Derby winner has ever sired a colt that also won?* —*Leo Cohen, Atlanta.*

A: Yes, several times, including one sequence of three generations: Reigh Count, the 1928 Kentucky Derby champion, sired Count Fleet (1943), whose son, Count Turf, won in 1951. Another notable father-son victory went to Pensive in 1944 and Ponder in 1949.

Q: *Some friends and I have been going to the Derby together for years. Talking about our 1975 trip we tried to remember the name of the character who used to cause such a stir at Churchill Downs by parading in velvet pants and fur top hats. This was at least twenty years ago, and the movie newsreel cameras would make him the center of the show. Would the people at the track know who this guy was, or is?* —*Joe Zollinger, Evansville, Indiana.*

A: You're thinking of the late "Diamond Jimmy" Moran, restaurateur, one-time prizefighter and bodyguard for Huey Long.

"Diamond Jimmy" would put on $110,000 worth of diamonds, including sparklers embedded in his two front teeth, on his shoelace tabs and his zipper pull. The cuff buttons on his coat were rubies with diamond initials spelling "Jimmy" on one wrist and "Moran" on the other. He would put on a mink tie and pink-dyed beaver top hat, then say, "You know, pal, you got to watch it. You could add one thing too much and ruin it all."

Q: *I'm always amazed that jockeys can stay on a horse when the stirrups are up around the horse's ears. In Europe the jocks have the stirrups almost normal length. Is the high ride an American fad, and how did it get started?* —*Eddie O., San Francisco.*

A: European courses often run uphill and downhill over uneven surfaces, so the rider needs the control of longer stirrups. American courses are uniformly flat.

Q: *How much does it really cost to own and race a racehorse? —Billy J., Sacramento.*

A: Most people think it's like J. P. Morgan's answer to a question about owning a yacht: "If you have to ask, you can't afford it." However, the tab of $9,000 for annual upkeep and training of a Thoroughbred is not beyond the affluence of today's swinging businessman. A bangtail is in the foreign sports car bracket.

Q: *I understand Secretariat's stud fee works out to about $19,000 per standing. Did Man O' War ever stand at stud, and if he did, what was his fee? —Elliott Fauchot, San Diego.*

A: Man O' War's fee, 1922 through 1924, was $2,500, but after his first get had shown their stuff on the racetrack as two-year-olds, the price went to $5,000.

Q: *I saw Mrs. Penny Tweedy on television talking to jockey Ron Turcotte in the paddock. She said something about him wearing new silks. I know about material and I find it hard to believe the shirts are made of silk, unless he has a dozen or so made up at a time. Do you know about this? —Emily Currington, Joplin, Missouri.*

A: Before World War I silk was traditionally used in Europe and that's how the term originated. Satin was used until the development of nylon, now the prevailing material. Silk will not withstand repeated washing.

Q: *Every year when the Kentucky Derby comes around, somebody brings up Willie Shoemaker's goof in pulling up his horse before the finish line. It's so taken for granted everyone knows the story, the details are omitted. What happened and did they do anything to Shoemaker? —Kenneth Petrie, Muncie, Indiana.*

A: First, no writer in the press box was aware that Shoemaker stood up in the stirrups just before the wire, easing Gallant Man into second place behind Willie Hartack and Iron Liege. A Churchill Downs steward, the late Lincoln Plant, alerted the writers to check the film patrol. Shoemaker at first denied his boner, saying the track was "wavy." He was set down for fifteen days. That same season Shoemaker had pulled up Swaps before the finish, allowing Porterhouse to win the California Stakes.

Q: *Can you give me some dollar-and-cents figures on owning a racehorse? I can't go it alone, but with three of my friends chipping in we might manage it. —Tony Sinopli, Yonkers, New York.*

A: The simplest way to buy a horse is at a claiming race, say, for $2,500. Then you must pay a trainer $20 to $30 a day to house, feed, and exercise the animal. This doesn't include veterinary bills. The jockey gets $35 to $50 per ride, plus 10 percent of what the horse wins (the trainer gets another 10 percent).

Most jocks will also expect you to have a win ticket going for them. You will spend between $4 and $25 for state license and a similar fee to register your colors. You must furnish the jockey his "silks" at a cost between $40 and $90. When the horse has to be rested, your fee at a farm will be $6 to $10 a day.

And for all this you may someday get your picture taken in the winner's circle.

Q: *I'm going to see the Indianapolis 500 for the first time. Are there any tips you can give me going in? —Ernest Herring, Darlington, South Carolina.*

A: A few: (1) Stay out of the infield—there are a lot of loose women in there. (2) Don't pick a fight with a guy in overalls. (3) Try to find a scalper who will sell you a seat on the backstretch between the third and fourth turns, where most of the fatalities occur. (Surely this is why you're going?) And (4) bring a portable radio with earplugs.

Q: *Race cars go so fast nowadays that the numbers don't seem to mean anything. I was wondering how long ago it was that the first winner of the Indy 500 averaged better than 100 miles an hour?* —*Morris Gibbons, Gardena, California.*

A: A driver named Peter De Paolo won the 1925 race with an average speed of 101.3 mph. What pushed him to break that historic barrier was the fact that De Paolo didn't realize he had lapped the second-place car. He raced it hubcap to hubcap, at full throttle, for several laps. His record time lasted, incidentally, until 1932.

Q: *I am an avid fisherman and just as avid in reading all of Ernest Hemingway. I have fished the Two-Hearted River in Upper Michigan which Hemingway described in his Nick Adams short stories. But it is nothing like he described and I have always thought he was meticulous about accuracy. Do you know if his river was merely a fiction, or has it been changed in some way?* —*Dr. F. J. Donleavy, Grand Rapids.*

A: Others have noticed that Hemingway's Two-Hearted and Michigan's are not the same. Fishermen have suspected the author did this deliberately to keep crowds from cluttering up his favorite fishing holes. Hemingway actually fished the Fox River. Literary critics believe he simply loved the name Two-Hearted River and used it under poetic license. It does have a sweeter ring than Fox.

Q: *I want to begin jogging to lose weight, but I have read a number of scare stories about it. Do you have an expert reference on jogging? I already have the approval of my family doctor.* —*Jim Amundsen, Gainesville, Florida.*

A: You should also see a foot doctor for his help in prescribing footwear. The more expensive the better, because real damage to ankles, shins, and knees may result if you're not careful. Other tips: Jog only on grass and never along a slanted surface. Also, running downhill is dangerous. If you can't afford expensive shoes, run barefoot on grass, which is the safest routine. Doctors disagree on a lot of things, including jogging, but all agree it will make the jogger "feel" better. In fact, it is addictive.

Q: *I am graduating with a journalism degree and campus experience in broadcasting. What do the professionals say in advising young people on how to get started in the sports end of the business?* —*Shep Bradford, Latrobe, Pennsylvania.*

A: The best tip we've heard, succinctly put, comes from Jack Craig, the *Boston Globe* columnist who comments on radio-TV sports: "Be satisfied to start with a low salary, stay single, stay loose, and know when to get out if you haven't made any progress within seven or eight years."

Q: *I am taking karate lessons and starting to get interested in everything that goes with it. Nobody here can tell me exactly what Kung Fu is, though we've all seen the TV program. Is it just blown up or imagined for a movie story, or what exactly is it?* —*Kenny Franklinton, Denver.*

A: Kung Fu is the original martial art (*wu-shu*) dating back to twenty-six centuries before Christ, in China. With all the Confucius talk brushed aside, its principles are simple—heightened concentration to get maximum force from the body, straight blows that never travel outside the width of the shoulders, and balance at all times. All of the other martial arts—judo, aikido, karate, and whatever—evolved from Kung Fu. An excellent book on all these subjects is available from Funk and Wagnalls: *Handbook of the Martial Arts and Self-Defense* (1975) by William Logan and Herman Petras.

Q: *An old-timer friend of mine calls free tickets Annie Oakleys, but he can't remember why. Do you know?* —*George B., San Francisco.*

A: Promoters punch holes in giveaway tickets so they won't have to pay tax on them. Annie Oakley, Irving Berlin's Get-Your-Gun girl, used to shoot holes in playing cards. But don't feel uninformed. When Babe Ruth was considering an offer from the Ziegfield Follies, a Yankee teammate asked if he could get him a couple of Annie Oakleys. "Kid," the Babe said, "if I go with the Follies, I'll get you all the broads you want."

Q: *In my church bulletin one Sunday there were divorce rates for different occupations, and professional athletes were near the bottom of the list. This surprised me, considering the money and the opportunity and the groupie temptations the fellows have. Has anyone suggested why there are comparably few divorces in the sports business? —Eleanor Velke, Pittsburgh.*

A: We have a few ideas why this is so. Many wives of pro stars have a "college sweetheart–campus hero" relationship with their husbands. They don't make as many demands, thus they keep their illusions longer. This attitude led to the classic examples of the marital alibis of pitcher Kirby Higbe and Gary Bell, decades apart. In Higbe's case, a love letter was mistakenly forwarded from the Brooklyn club offices to Higbe's home. Next day the players breathlessly waited to hear of the explosion. Higbe reported there was none. "What did you tell her?" they asked. "Oh," he said, "I just told her it must be some other Kirby Higbe." Then there was Bell's roommate, who handled a 5:00 A.M. call from Mrs. Bell and said, "He's not here, Nan. He's out playing golf." The latter story would never have come out, if Mrs. Bell hadn't delighted in telling it.

Q: *I saw Howard Cosell get kissed by Billie Jean King on television and he said, "I wish this was an X-rated show." My question is, did Howard know what he was saying? —Karen Camp, Boston.*

A: Never mind what he said, he knew what he meant. By Howard's standards, that kiss made it an X-rated show. He leads a sedate social life. More startling than the kiss was Billie Jean telling a national television audience that she and her husband agreed they should never have married, they should have lived together instead.

Q: *My cousin and I would like to know the rules and regulations for making a world record in pogo stick jumping. Could we take turns jumping, and if we fall or something would we have to quit? How do we get the record recorded? —Lynda and Teresa, Brooklyn, Mississippi.*

A: The *Guiness Book of World Records* has become the clearing house for all such zany behavior. They say submission of a record should be accompanied by "newspaper clippings, radio or television reports, a signed authentication by an independent adult individual or representative of an organization of standing in the community." We checked with Guiness and the chap said it is highly unlikely the firm would recognize a partnership record in pogo stick jumping. If you want to try, however, send everything to: Guiness Superlatives, Ltd., 2 Cecil Court, London Road, Enfield, Middlesex, England.

Q: *I would like to know the fastest sport in the world. —Mehul Sheth, Caldwell, New Jersey.*

A: Free-fall speeds of 614 mph have been recorded in sky diving competition. Fastest athlete on terra firma was hockey star Bobby Hull, clocked at 29.7 mph, which is a fraction faster than the Olympic record for 500 meters. Fastest "ball" in a moving game, including a hockey puck, is the pelota used in jai alai, going 190 mph. A golf ball driven off a tee has been timed at 170 mph. We hope that somewhere in all this you have the answer to your question.

Q: *Back in the late 1920s there was a great race-horse, owned by Samuel B. Riddle, called Man O' War, which in his career won twenty out of twenty-one races. Please let me know the name of the horse that defeated him. —Harry Fisher, West Palm Beach.*

A: Most racing fans can remember the answer to

126

this one because Big Red ran second to a steed aptly named Upset. That was August 13, 1919, in the Sanford Memorial Stakes at Saratoga. What few fans know, however, is that Man O' War ran the fastest six furlongs of his career that day (1:11 1/5).

Q: *In the movie* The Sting *the whole plot was about sandbagging a big gambler, and they used the words "passing the post." I understand what happened in the movie, but it wasn't clear what "passing the post" meant. Can you explain, please?* —Marie L., Indianapolis.

A: Handbooks, whose wonderful off-track betting institutions, often allow bettors the opportunity to wager on a race past post time as a convenience—and to get as much money through the windows as possible. Post time is recorded the instant the horses leave the starting gate. Remember, the clientele in a handbook are betting on races across the country, in different time zones, and they are sealed off from the outside world. "Passing the post" on a bookie means betting on a winner after the race has been run, an irresistible temptation. It has been done, but in some circles it can cost a fellow a kneecap. In New Orleans, when a guy says somebody "passed the post" on him, he means he got hit when he wasn't looking.

Q: *What's the record payoff for a $2 win ticket? I'm betting it was at Caliente.* —Anthony R., Atlanta.

A: You're close, by an oddity. In 1934 Old Kickapoo went off at Caliente without the backing of a single win ticket, and won. The win pool was put into the place money, and Kickapoo paid $230.40 in that spot. The highest-priced winner of all time was Wishing Ring at Latonia, Kentucky, in 1912, when five lucky backers got $1,884 each.

Q: *I understand you have to report gambling winnings on your income tax. How does this work at the racetrack? Sign me, Concerned—(Name withheld), Atlanta.*

A: Racetracks are supposed to furnish Internal Revenue with the name of a winner who collects $600 or more on one bet.

Q: *I am down $128 on eight races and I am sitting here wondering how the $2 bet came into existence. Why not $1 or $3? —Ed Beardsley, San Francisco.*

A: The original pari-mutuel bet, from 1878 to 1911, was $5. In the latter year Colonel Matt Winn introduced the $2 ticket at Churchill Downs, and the compromise sum, not too cheap and not too dear, was an instant success. William Riggs of Pimlico visited the Kentucky plant and brought the innovation to northern tracks.

Q: *A tennis friend of mine tells me that Ilie Nastase is getting a divorce. He is some hunk of Hungarian and I'm interested in hearing about it. Do you know the story? —Emilie Aucoin, Vancouver, B.C.*

A: Nastase, actually a rowdy Rumanian, is a carefree joker whose words are never engraved on stone. This rumor resulted from a press conference when Nastase was asked if he'd play on the World Championship Tennis tour one year. "Next year?" he said. "I may get divorced and remarried and divorced again next year. Don't ask me about next year." Wife Dominique was in the audience and laughed along with everyone else.

Q: *What is your opinion of Jimmy Connors? —Cliff Rietten, Charlotte, North Carolina.*

A: Young, talented, spoiled. But that's not a bad combination for success in the world today. Aside from his determination to win both Wimbledon and Forest Hills again, Connors has show business ambitions. His agent, Bill Riordan, says that famed songwriter Paul Anka ("My Way," plus a dozen other hits) is writing a song for Connors, who has a pleasant voice but no volley. Connors also intends to pursue a dramatic

128

career eventually. Maybe then he will get off his current act, "Peck's Bad Boy."

Q: *What is the matter with Arthur Ashe? Sometimes he looks like a world-beater, but he always folds at crucial times. What is his problem? —Arnold Cantrell, Baltimore.*

A: First, Ashe's own view: "Rosewall is a better player than me, surely for one match. Laver is still better, and so are Nastase and Newcombe. But I am just this tiny bit away from them. Smith and Okker probably rate with me—in the second echelon. Dr. Walter Johnson of Lynchburg, Virginia, taught me to play tennis, but he never taught me to serve and volley. It wasn't his own style, and he said I would get it in time. And the serve I did get. But I never could get the volley. It's a touch shot, and I guess I was too old to pick it up naturally by the time I started trying, around age sixteen or so."

The pros' view of Arthur's trouble is simple: he is just too nice a fellow, lacking the aggressive ingredient all the great champions have by nature.

Q: *Can you tell me the origin of the term "seeded" that is used in tennis to give top-ranked players a better place in a tournament? Unless it's a corruption of the word "ceded," I can't figure it out. —Louise Greuning, Dayton.*

A: This quaint analogy originated in England and refers to the way you plan a garden, by "seeding" flowers here and there for an orderly and attractive growth.

Q: *Does Dean Martin have two sons, a good one and a bad one? I read that Dean Martin, Jr., signed with the WFL Portland Storm, and then I read that Dino Martin is in court for possessing machine guns and bazookas. —Ed Cunningham, San Jose.*

A: They are one and the same. Dino's guilty plea to possession of illegal weapons did not keep him from trying out as a wide receiver with the Storm. His tennis buddy, Jimmy Connors, volunteered this insight on young Martin: "Rich kids like that get new Ferraris every year, but they aren't responsible people. Never show up on time, forget their friends. Dino wanted to bet me always. He had a famous father and several tons of dough and time on his hands and all the broads. Yet all he wanted to do was play good tennis."

Q: *Jimmy Demaret was the most colorful golf professional for a period of some thirty years. His last prominent sports role was as an announcer at golf tournaments. He hasn't been mentioned at all for a long time. As an announcer he was still colorful and I would like to know why he disappeared from the scene. —Harry Krug, Juno Beach, Florida.*

A: Demaret, who more than any man brought fashion to the golf links, long ago reached a point where he no longer needed the work or the travel. After seven years as an analyst on All-Star Golf, and four more on Shell's Wonderful World of Golf, Jimmy turns down the occasional offers that still come his way. He divides his time between three Texas courses, Onion Creek in Austin, which he designed and joint-ventured with Time-Life, Valley Inn at Brownsville, and Houston's famed Champions. He has a financial interest in all three.

Q: *Please tell me what you know about Johnny Miller taking off for long stretches from the pro golf tour. Maybe it's because he was so much in the headlines, but it doesn't seem like other top players stay away for weeks at a time. —Jake D'Angelo, Passaic, New Jersey.*

A: Miller is indeed unique in scheduling his tour action to include long layoffs. Oddly enough, baseball Hall of Famer Ralph Kiner has a theory about this, with which many of Miller's fellow pros agree. "Miller has to do that because he doesn't drink. He's a teetotaler. Nobody can take that kind of day-after-day

130

pressure on the tour without an occasional belt to relax. It's either that or get away from it entirely. So Miller drops out." The Mormon parbuster also has his sights set on the major titles and is gearing his game to the Masters and the Open. He won eleven tournaments in a fourteen-month stretch and he's tired of hearing, "Yeah, but Miller only won one big one in his life."

Q: *Can you give me some facts about Ivory Crockett, the great sprinter from Southern Illinois. How tall is he? Where does he live? How does he support himself? And is Ivory his real name?* —Artena Davis, Detroit.

A: Crockett is a little big man at 5-7, has worked full-time for the IBM office in Peoria, Illinois, where his proud bosses generously arrange his schedule to allow time for workouts. When he returned from his record nine-flat effort at Modesto in 1975, a sign was hung from his office window: "Ivory Crockett Works Here." As for his unusual name, Ivory says: "I guess my mother was doing a lot of dishes when she was expecting me."

Q: *What does "pari-mutuel" mean, exactly? Does it have something to do with the computer-way odds are figured for the track payoffs?* —Yvonne S., Milwaukee.

A: The name does sound mathematical, but actually it's a version of "Paris Mutual," the original system as invented by Pierre Oller and used at Longchamps in 1872.

Q: *Can you tell me what are the requirements to get on the pro bowling tour?* —Eddie Iola, Boston.

A: First you must have an accredited average of 190 for the past three years. Next a letter of recommendation from a Professional Bowlers Association member in your area. Then apply to your regional PBA office, whose address you can get from a bowling proprietor. One other item—you'll need about $20,000 to bankroll you for expenses through one season.

Q: *Watching the TV coverage of the national swimming finals at Kansas City, I noticed two or three of the men had shaved their heads. I understand they even shave their armpits. Has it ever been established that this really does let them swim faster? —Dale Irby, Joplin, Missouri.*

A: We referred your question to the best source we could find: Mark Spitz. "If they think it helps," said the 1972 Olympics hero, "it helps." But no one who saw Spitz shaggy and mustachioed, win seven gold medals at Munich can believe that the hairless look has any scientific edge. The Russians, incidentally, were fascinated by Mark's moustache. They asked if it didn't cause drag or friction. Resorting to a bit of gamesmanship, Spitz told them no, "It acts as a kind of shield. The water slides off it and stays out of my mouth, and I can go faster." Observers at later international events noted that some Soviet swimmers were sporting full beards.

Q: *I have great respect for young Kyle Rote and his religious beliefs, and it pleased me to see him with the Superstars' title again. But I wonder how he justifies the life-style of so many athletes today? What is his opinion of someone like Joe Namath, whose values seem to be the opposite of Rote's? —Aaron Minshew, Tampa.*

A: A divinity student, Kyle Jr., nonetheless understands and enjoys the rough camaraderie of sports. At one Superstars' competition, whenever Rote passed by, shotputter Brian Oldsfield would ask loudly, "What's a Bible?" Responds Rote: "I don't run around preaching to people or to my teammates. You can impress people more by the way you live, the way you act."

Rote has a sense of humor of his own. He feels the Namath image grew out of the old AFL's need for a homegrown star. "It snowballed and was overplayed," says Kyle. "Like that *Playboy* interview that had Joe saying he slept with 350 girls in Alabama. That made me think he was a better athlete than I thought he was."

SUMMER

Someone once said that baseball was great, if you had enough Sominex. He was wrong. The pace of baseball is its charm and strength. In no other sport do we get to know the players so well. We meet them every day. And the names, how they fascinate us. Ty. Pie. Babe. DiMag. Van Lingle Mungo. And Mickey Mantle. There was a great baseball name. Not just a good baseball name. A great baseball name. He had speed and power and he played in pain. And there was something else. He may have been the only player who ever lived who, even after he made the Hall of Fame, still heard people talking about his potential.

Mickey Mantle:
The Baseball Player

Everyone knew the sad story of Mickey Mantle. Great player. Bad head. He was the last Yankee to win the Triple Crown—average, homers, RBI—but since then he's won the Triple Crown of Suckers. This guy can bust you into bankruptcy in anything you name— bowling alley, food franchise, clothing stores.

With the calm acceptance of a man who has lived through false stories more hairy than that, Mantle says: "People thought I was destitute."

Well, they don't think so any more. Seemingly all of a sudden, after eight years out of the game, Mantle in 1976 had become one of the sports world's hottest commercial images. He was on the tube more than Cincinnati Reds' star Pete Rose, including playoffs.

You see him dwarfed by two fungi-troubled feet, pitching MP-27: "I've seen a whole lot of scratchin' going on." A little later, in the middle of "Police Story," here he comes at you again as "Mickey Mantle, Executive," and singing yet: "Brylcreem a little dab'll do ya—for men who use their head about their hair." If you hang on for the "Late Show," he'll get you again, this time co-starred with old pal Whitey Ford: "Can you imagine where we'd be right now if they had Miller lite beer in our day?" And Whitey makes a grand gesture to reply, "Sure, Mickey, we'd be in the Beer Drinkers' Hall of Fame."

He does similar shots for Brut and Bow Wow Dog Food ("Nutrition for the active dog"), and when viewers in New York State see his good old country-boy face, they know a plug for Carvel Ice Cream is coming on. Whitey's in that one, too.

What's more, the commercials are only the tip of the iceberg in an industry that should have been known as "They Love Mickey, Incorporated." How did all this come about? The answer is partly because he finally landed in the hands of an astute young Dallas attorney, partly because Mantle worked at it with skills few suspected he possessed, but mainly simply because Mickey Mantle is Mickey Mantle.

Mantle turned forty-four in October, 1976. He was still trim. The torso still sloped from those massive shoulders to hips that belonged on a welterweight fighter, suggesting as always both power and grace. He was, you remember, the classic home run hitter and also the fastest man ever clocked from the left-side batter's box to first base. That's what he was. What he is now is impressive in its own way.

Sitting in his expansive and beautifully appointed home (pool, cabana, trophy room, humming bird feeder) in a Dallas suburb, Mantle supplies a matter-of-fact reason for all his recent success with TV commercials.

"About three years ago," he says, "some advertising people got up a survey about athletes. They had one category on who do you believe—Stan Musial got that, but I was second—and they had another on who do you recognize. Namath took that one, but I didn't finish far behind. It turned out that no matter what question they asked, I was right up there at the top."

Mantle is without rancor when he remarks, "As far as making money, Dallas has been horseshit for me. Nobody knows I even live there, and next year will be our twentieth year in the same house. I can go anywhere in Dallas and not be bothered a bit. I can't go on the street in New York without collecting a mob. Every time I've been on a plane coming home, I get to talking to people, and like I say everytime, they'll say, 'What are you going to Dallas for? You got a speaking engagement?'"

The first business fall Mantle took was with a bowling alley in a basement at Exchange Park, near the end of his playing career. "They were going to give it to Doak Walker," he recalls, "but Doak was having some kind of family problem, so they asked me to take it. It never paid off and we sold it to some people from New Jersey."

When he retired in 1968, food franchises using celebrity names were the new bonanza. His was "Mickey Mantle's Country Cookin'." Mantle says, "I told people I had a great slogan for the restaurants— 'The best piece of chicken you can get unless you're a rooster.' Those kind of ideas are probably what put us out of business."

For a while there, though, it looked like Mantle had made the fortune his partners had promised him. "The stock went to $15 a share and I had 110,000 shares, but there was a clause in there I didn't know about, where I couldn't sell mine, but everybody else could sell theirs." He is not bitter as he dredges up these memories; in fact, hardly even rueful.

After the burnt country cookin', there was a men's clothing store in Atlanta that didn't sell clothes, and a firm in New York City that furnished part-time employees, "Mantle's Men and Namath's Girls." This company later merged with an established employment agency, which could only use the athletes' names for one year.

It was about this time that everyone believed all of Mantle's hard-earned Yankee money had gone kaput. The average fan doesn't understand that athletes seldom if ever put any of their own bankroll into such ventures. They simply lend their names.

"Yeah," says Mantle, "but that hurts, too. Pretty soon they say, 'My God, is Mantle in it? It'll never go.' "

About the time Mantle was trying to extricate himself from the food franchise, he took the suggestion of some friends and engaged attorney Roy True, now thirty-eight, a partner in the firm of True and Zable, specializing in corporate and business practice. "I wouldn't walk around the corner to a Little League banquet," Mantle says, "if Roy didn't tell me it was okay."

A big block of the Mantle income today comes from Charles Sammons' Reserve Life Insurance Company, a Dallas firm. "I'm the V-P in charge of special markets," Mantle says, "which is public relations, I guess. It's a billion-dollar company. I made a phonograph record for them on 'How to Hit' for your Little Leaguers. They got 250,000 of them and sent them out to the agents. Any potential customer wants one he can get it. Then the agent brings it to him and starts the pitch about insurance."

In between the commercials and the sales meetings for Reserve Life, Mantle regularly makes appearances for companies such as Allied Chemical and Xerox and the E-Z Rider Cigarette Paper Company of Atlanta— you name it. He gets a minimum of $2,500 for each of these, plus expenses, and sometimes as much as $4,000. Allied Chemical has an annual golf trip for their executives, and Mantle joins them for four days of sport and a lot of laughs. That's a $4,000 job, and one he thoroughly enjoys. His golf handicap places him as a mid-70s shooter.

Mantle, through Roy True, turns down about 90 percent of the requests he gets. Some are refused on the basis of credibility, such as a body-building machine of questionable value or a therapeutic bathtub water swirler without medical evidence to back up its claims.

"The fact is," Mantle says, "I've made more money the last three or four years than I ever did with the Yankees, and I made $100,000 a year my last seven years with the Yankees."

Mantle is proud of his home, which will be paid off in 1977, and proudest of a trophy room addition engineered by his wife Merlyn, a stunning blonde who has given Mantle four strapping sons and still maintains the figure of a teenager. One eight-foot wall is covered with magazine covers devoted to Mantle, and a long wall has enough photos of Mantle-cum-celebrities to furnish two Toots Shor restaurants. One shows him hugging the neck of one-time Yankee pitcher Jim Bouton, who later wrote a tattletale book (*Ball Four*) that revealed Mantle was human. "If Merlyn knew who that was," Mantle said, grinning, "I think she'd throw it in the can."

And there is a crammed four-by-six-foot glass trophy case, including a 600-foot tape measure supposedly used to check the distance of a 585-foot home run he hit against Washington in 1956. "Those three MVP plaques," Mantle said, "are the big deals in there." There is also a gold record of Teresa Brewer's song, "I Love Mickey."

The young Mickey was a switch-hitting phenom schooled by his daddy, a coal miner, in Commerce, Oklahoma. He was an all-around athlete. "I had a football scholarship to OU," he recalls, "but a Yankee scout came down and offered me a $1,200 bonus, plus $300 if I'd play out the summer in the K-M-O (Kansas-Missouri-Oklahoma) League. I did it and that blew the OU deal. Hell, everybody wanted to play for the Yankees then. [The scout was Tom Greenwade, who had discovered an earlier talent named Lou Gehrig.] The first fifteen years I was in the majors, I played in thirteen World Series. That'll never happen again, because of the draft. I started out as a shortstop. My first spring training with the Yankees they looked at me there for a couple of games and they said, 'Hell, this kid is an outfielder if he's any damn thing'."

As it turned out, Mantle played only one season with the fellow from whom he'd take the baton as the next great centerfielder, Joe DiMaggio, in 1951. "He had always been my idol," Mantle says, "but that year I was with him I didn't know when to speak to him. He was so aloof and reserved."

In a twist of fate no scriptwriter would ever dare, DiMaggio and Willie Mays were involved in a single play which affected Mantle's career decidedly and ultimately cut it short by a season or a few. "It was the Series in 1951," Mantle says, "and Mays hit a pop fly. I was in rightfield, DiMaggio in center. As soon as the ball came off his bat, I knew there was no way Joe could get to it, so I hauled ass. Just before I got there, I heard Joe say, 'I got it.' He was *camped* under it. I put on the brakes and the back spikes of my right foot caught on the rubber cover of a sprinkler head. This bone here"—Mantle put a hand on his right kneecap —"went all the way through there"—and Mantle's hand scooted outward toward a coffee table. Who knows what the man would have been had that not happened? All of his great records came afterward.

Mantle has cause to have no regrets about the injury, or his career which he abandoned at thirty-five. "I played in the best place there was to play," he says. "New York. Why, we had fifteen sportswriters from New York papers on the road with us, and that's not counting the guys who were doing magazine articles or radio shows. I've always said, long before Aaron broke Ruth's home run record, that Aaron was the forgotten player of our time—the Mantle and Mays era. He was doing the same thing Willie and I were doing, but he was stuck off out in Milwaukee."

There is no yen in Mantle for a return to the game in some other capacity, say as manager. "Lord, no," he says. "I do better than any of the managers and I don't have to worry about getting fired. Also, I don't have to travel eight months out of the year at a stretch. I go down to spring training with the Yankees for two weeks every spring and help them out, and I appear at all the special days they have. That's enough for me."

If you talk about the "Pride of the Yankees," it comes out in a long conversation with Mantle, bit by bit. Along the way, you will drag out of him a historic point. "I hit a home run off Barney Schultz in the '64 Series against the Cardinals that was the sixteenth World Series home run I'd hit. That broke Babe Ruth's record of fifteen. I went on later to hit two others, and I think that's a record that will last awhile, because nobody else is goin' to be in thirteen World Series his first fifteen years. Also, I played in more games as a Yankee than anybody else, 2,400. That's a hundred more than Lou Gehrig."

Mantle had given the impression most of his career that the pressure of being a great star was something to which he could not adjust. In the early years especially, he was surly and suspicious and a tough interview.

But age and a taste of the second division changed all that, as oft it will. "All my years with the Yankees," he says, "it seems like every season I was going for something, like the home run title or the batting championship, or else the team was in a pennant race. I had a whole bunch of people after my locker after every game. I used to look over at the other fellows—they were only talking about where to go out that night—and I'd think, 'Gee, I wish I had a season where I didn't have to put up with all of this. Where I could be just talking to the guys about where we're going to get together.'

"Well, after they fired Yogi [Berra] and brought in Johnny Keane—a deal I don't understand to this day—I got my wish. I had a bad year, the Yankees had a bad year. I think we finished tenth, at least that's how I remembered it. That's when I decided I liked the 'pressure' a lot more than I thought I did."

If Mantle misses anything today, it is the locker room camaraderie. "You lived with those guys for eight months, and when you've finally got to leave them, a part of you dies. Remember, I had to retire at thirty-five."

In a curious way, his name was dropped as a prospect for the manager's job of the original Rangers by former Texan owner Bob Short. Then rumors spread that Mantle was out hustling golf bets at Preston Trail, a tightly knit, all-male Dallas golf club of 200 members. The memory bites. "He [Short] never called me, in the first place, which I couldn't care less," Mantle says, "but then came the rumor. I wouldn't be acceptable for the Rangers because I was a 'golf hustler' at Preston

141

Trail. Lordy, if anything it was the other way around. I always accuse those guys of hustling me. That's what the first tee is all about."

Mantle's attorney, Roy True, doesn't regard the current Mantle prosperity as an "accident." He believes it's a case of untapped assets and unrealized character coming to the fore. "When Mickey and I first started out together, getting him untangled from the food franchise, everybody told me I ought to make sure Mantle's name was kept before the public or they'd forget him. This didn't make sense to me. How is anybody going to forget Mickey Mantle? Remember, Mickey is essentially a shy and retiring person, a layback type of guy. We pick his appearances carefully. We accepted a brief role on the 'Game of the Week.' Little by little, Mick became acquainted with the TV medium. He listened to recordings of his voice, and he schooled himself to enunciate more clearly. He saw when he made a positive impression and when he didn't.

"And it turned out that he was a quick study. When I first got dates for filming commercials, the producers would tell me, 'Better get this guy in a day ahead of time so we can work with him.' I knew this was ridiculous. Mick went in the day of the commercial and in fifteen minutes he had it cold. What's more, he had patience—which you need a lot of when you work with those people. I had producers call me later and say, 'Mickey's tremendous. You can't believe the trouble we've had with other jocks.'"

True has since been asked by his friends to explain the considerable success of Mantle as a lodestone commercial quantity. "I tell them," True says, "that it's because Mantle is a legitimate folk hero, a guy from a deprived background, a coal miner in Oklahoma, who made it big in America. But underneath is the layer that he is a regular guy and he is a good guy. One of the endearing qualities to me about Mickey is that he trusts people. He'll call me some morning and say, 'I met a helluva guy last night. A terrific guy. He says he's going to make me ten million dollars. Will you talk

142

to him?' Now that appeals to me, as a lawyer, all day writing contracts that spell out to the last 'T' what anybody can or cannot do—and still you got to go to court at the end of the hassle. Not with Mickey. He believes."

True sees another odd virtue in his client: "He is on no ego trip. He was invited to the White House by President Ford on the occasion of the visit by the President of France, Giscard d'Estaing. First of all, he was upset by the fact that he had to wear tails. But most of all, he said, 'I don't understand this deal—why in the world do they want me up there? Do I really have to go?' It turned out he sat at the same table with the President, who made him feel right at home, and Merlyn sat at a table with Nelson Rockefeller, who was extremely gracious to her. When Mickey got back, he called and said, 'Well, you were right. I wouldn't have believed it, but we had the time of our life.' "

Mantle, even to this day, remains an immense presence to anyone who recalls him as the first great coast-to-coast TV baseball star. What memories he must have, to warm him through the winter nights.

Not so.

"I was sitting here the other day," Mantle says, "and I tried to remember what it was like to hit a home run and win a game. And I couldn't remember. It was like the whole thing happened to somebody else."

Questions & Answers

Q: *I saw where a player was "looking dead red" when he hit a home run. I have never heard this expression before. Can you explain it? —Jim Keough, Carbondale, Illinois.*

A: It means he was anticipating a fastball, and it's a natural descendant of the old term "fireballer." The new breed of player has added to the game's vocabulary the last few years. For example: A home run is a dinger. A home-run hitter is a guy who can jack it out of here. A no-hitter is a no-no. The game of baseball is simply ball, as in, "He's the best third baseman in ball." When a rainsquall passes, the players are in for nine. A fast runner is a guy who can hike it, a slick fielder is one who can pick it, and our old fireballer is a pitcher who brings it.

Q: *My son wrote a fan letter to Mike Marshall, (then) of the Dodgers, and never received a reply. Later, I heard Marshall tell an interviewer that he doesn't give advice to kids. I don't understand this. Don't big league players realize they have an obligation to help promote the game? —Mrs. Calvin Faulkner, Charlotte, North Carolina.*

A: The scholarly relief pitcher does give advice. He urges youngsters not to pitch every day and not to experiment with trick pitches. What he won't do is tell them how HE does it. "On national television one season," he says, "I demonstrated how to throw a screwball. I specifically warned that no youngster under the age of fifteen should attempt to place his arm in this position because of possible injury. Immediately, I was deluged with letters from kids saying how they were working on their screwball and would I please tell them more."

He didn't, and he won't.

Q: *I have written to several different people in reference to my question, but with no reply. I would like to know who made up the seventh inning stretch, and why? —Dave Espinosa, San Bernardino, California.*

A: The tradition dates back to an opening day appearance at the Washington ball park by the then president, William Howard Taft, in the years before World War I. A portly gentleman, President Taft rose to adjust himself between halves of the seventh inning. The fans around him, curious, stood to look at the nation's chief executive. Soon the entire stadium was standing. One way or another, it caught on.

Q: *Would you list the top ten shutout pitchers of all time, and who holds the record for one season?* —*Dr. Robert M. Baker, Berlin, Maryland.*

A: In order, the run-less leaders are: (1) Walter Johnson (113); (2) Grover Cleveland Alexander (90); (3) Christy Mathewson (83); (4) Cy Young (77); (5) Eddie Plank (64); (6) Warren Spahn (63); (7) Ed Walsh (58); (8) Pud Galvin (57); (9) Bob Gibson (56); (10) Juan Marichal (52).

The record for one season was established by Alexander for the Phillies with sixteen shutouts in 1916, the same year the American League record of nine was being set by none other than Babe Ruth. The all-time record for a left-hander belongs to Sandy Koufax, Dodgers, with eleven in 1963.

Q: *Every chance he gets, Howard Cosell knocks baseball. Do you know what his gripe is, or does he feel he has to do it because he's on "Monday Night Football?"* —*Gregory Hesse, Raleigh, North Carolina.*

A: Cosell lost whatever enthusiasm he had for baseball when the Dodgers and the Giants abandoned New York for the West Coast. But his current complaint involves what he feels is a double standard, as exercised by the hearings in Congress led by Torbert MacDonald.

"I still find it unbelievable," says Howard, "that baseball, alone among all the major sports, is immune from the antitrust laws. In pro football, over forty players have moved to other teams of their own initiative in the last five years. In baseball, only one, Curt Flood. Yet Torbert MacDonald can call Pete Rozelle a demagogue, and ask Bowie Kuhn how the designated hitter is working out."

Q: *What was it about the late Danny Murtaugh that the Pirates always brought him back as manager? I*

*know he got a Series for them, but nobody else got that
kind of allegiance. —Cornell F., Pottstown, Pennsylvania.*

A: Murtaugh and Joe Brown went back a long way,
back in fact to the 50s when Brown was G. M. and
Murtaugh the manager of the New Orleans Pelicans.
Old times are thicker than water. Incidentally, the second baseman on those Pelican teams was Earl Weaver,
lately American League manager of the year.

Q: *All the stories about Casey Stengel made him
sound like the most beloved figure since Santa Claus.
But I can remember when some of his former Yankee
players knocked him hard. Since they won all the time,
what was the basis of their beef against Stengel?
—Chet Lieber, Lincoln, Nebraska.*

A: No one ever doubted that Casey was human. He
had his faults, and one was that he could be rough and
impatient with young players. He once gave outfielder
Norm Siebern a chewing-out that was so rough, some
baseball people later insisted it was what ruined Siebern. He could be cruel in his assessments of others.
Of Jimmy Piersall, who had a history of eccentric behavior, he said: "He's great but you gotta play him in
a cage." His view of straight-as-an-arrow Bobby Rich-
ardson: "He doesn't smoke, doesn't drink, doesn't run
around with girls and doesn't stay out late, and he still
can't hit .250."

Q: *Sports lost a great lady when Joan Whitney Payson died. Casey Stengel may have made the Mets a
household word, but it was her money and her determination that made them a success. Her two great loves
were horses and baseball. Other than that you read very
little about her. Is there a story behind how she became
the owner of the Mets? —Christopher Rauch, Palm
Springs.*

A: Mrs. Payson was recruited by Bill Shea to be
one of the owners of a New York franchise in a pro-
posed third major league, the Continental League. But

Shea, a New York attorney, was really using that as leverage to get an expansion franchise in the National League. The strategy paid off, and when the Mets were born, Mrs. Payson was the obvious choice to own them.

A lifelong Giants' fan, and a frequent spectator at the big fights, she and her brother, Jock Whitney, owned the Greentree Stable, whose colors were once worn by Tom Fool, among other champions. But the Mets became her great obsession. She spent most of their first summer in Greece, being advised each day by telegram of the latest Mets' outcome. As the losses piled up, she notified the club by wire: PLEASE TELL US ONLY WHEN METS WIN. "That was about the last word I heard from America that summer," she once recalled.

Q: *When I was a youngster, I read a great baseball story about three outfielders who all had red hair. Now I would like my boy to read it. Can you help me track it down? —George Seifert, Boise.*

A: Ask your librarian for a collection of short stories that includes "The Redheaded Outfield" by Zane Grey. The great Western author once played professional baseball before riding the Purple Sage. His classic story—featuring Red Gilbat, Reddy Clammer, and centerfielder Reddie Ray—climaxed with the incomparable Ray having to play the entire outfield by himself.

Q: *Ever since I was a kid, I have thought pitchers were paranoid about their arms, wearing their warm-up jackets with only one arm inside, putting on a jacket when they were base runners, and so on. Is this an old-time idea, or do modern pitchers still regard their arms as precious? —Ken Ridglea, Boise.*

A: Any pitcher has good reason to be psychotic about his meal ticket. Most veteran pitchers can't straighten their throwing arms at the elbow. Tiny ruptures of blood vessels are the medical reason a pitcher shouldn't throw without three days' rest. It's natural to take elaborate precautions. For example, NY Mets star Tom Seaver has always insisted wife Nancy sleep on the left side of the bed—so she won't roll over on his arm during the night. Seaver said he once woke up with his arm "asleep" and nearly had a nervous breakdown.

Q: *Can you tell me who started the ball players' term "the World Serious," or how long the expression has been in use? —Herbert Kingsley, Fort Wayne.*

A: Ring Lardner, Sr., author of *Alibi Ike* and the classic short story "Haircut," had his fictional ball players refer to the World Series that way, circa 1923.

Q: *I have two questions concerning Jackie Robinson. First, who preceded him at second base? At the time Jackie was playing, who were the regular outfielders? Concerning Roy Campanella, what was his age when he had his terrible accident? —Mike Penkrot, Scott AFB, Illinois.*

A: The Brat, Eddie Stanky, was the Dodger second baseman when Jackie Robinson reached Brooklyn in 1947. Robinson played first base that year, moved to second when Stanky was sold to the Braves next season. Pete Reiser in center and Dixie Walker in right were outfield regulars, with Gene Hermanski and Al Gionfriddo sharing left field.

The great Dodger catcher, Campanella, was thirty-six when his rented Chevy spun out of control on an icy road in January of 1958 and crashed into a telephone pole, paralyzing him from the neck down.

Q: *There was a song that got popular a while back made up almost entirely, I think, of the names of baseball players. Can you find out the name of the song and who wrote it? —Ginger Marcus, San Pedro, California.*

A: You're thinking of a song entitled "Van Lingle Mungo," written by David Frishberg. The words are, basically, just the names of ball players out of the composer's childhood, sung one after the other in a kind of lilting refrain: Whitey Kurowski, Johnny Sain,

Eddie Joost, Johnny Pesky, Ferris Fain, Van Lingle Mungo . . . Kind of gets you, doesn't it?

Q: *I know the name of a player who was in the major leagues when Babe Ruth was playing and still there when Hank Aaron started playing. I'll send you guys a cigar if you can find him. —(No name), Gary, Indiana.*

A: Send Panatellas. Since you're in the White Sox–Cubs territory we checked there first and got him. Phil Cavarretta, first baseman for the Cubs and onetime NL batting champion and MVP, began his career in 1934, a year before Ruth retired, and ended it in 1955, the year after Aaron began.

Q: *I have been a Dizzy Dean fan all my life from the time he started with the Cardinals. I even listened to him broadcast the Browns' games though I wasn't a Browns' fan. I have collected all the stories about him since his death and am compiling "favorite" stories about him. Do you know of one that hasn't been included in all the obituaries? —Ollie Heinemann, St. Louis.*

A: Our favorite dates back to Dizzy's service in the army at age sixteen in Fort Sam Houston, where he had a job shoveling manure from the horse corral. An officer demanded to know when Dizzy was going to deliver manure for his flower garden and Diz replied, "Right away, sir. You are number two on my manure list."

Q: *Was Dizzy Dean known as "Dizzy" before he got to the big leagues? If not, how did he get that name? —Tony Carroll, Long Beach, California.*

A: Dizzy was born Jay Hanna Dean, changed his two front names to Jerome Herman at age seven when a childhood friend of that name died. The "Dizzy" was hung on him by Chicago White Sox third-base coach Lena Blackburne in a 1930 spring game at Houston. He struck out eighteen White Sox as Blackburne screamed, "You're letting that dizzy kid make a fool out of you. Are you gonna take that from this dizzy kid?"

Q: *Everybody who has kept up with baseball a long time knows that Dizzy Dean's career was ended because Earl Averill's drive hit him on the toe in the All-Star game. I have read this many times, but never have I read why Dizzy was dumb enough to start pitching again before the toe was healed, ruining his arm. Did he ever explain this? —Hal Mahon, Detroit.*

A: The tragedy was a result of avarice, callous handling, and competitive ignorance. Cardinal boss Branch Rickey highly appreciated Dizzy as the game's greatest drawing card and kept him with the team. When Manager Frank Frisch asked Dizzy if he was ready to pitch, Dean recalled, "The toe was stickin' out of my shoe with a splint on it, but when somebody asked me would I pitch, I could never say no."

Q: *In the stories about Dizzy Dean's death I was surprised to see he won only 150 games and yet he is in the Hall of Fame. Did Dean just make it on his personality? There are a lot of pitchers with better records. —Stan Curry, Norfolk, Virginia.*

A: Until Dean's career was curtailed by a freak on-field injury, he had 120 wins in five seasons, an average of 24 a year. His 30–7 record in 1934 is the last time a National League pitcher hit that number. Also, there was glory about Dizzy on the mound that is not transmitted by statistics.

Q: *I would like to know the name of the first American athlete to sign a contract for $100,000 for one year or one season period, any sport. —Terry Rice, Wyoming, Michigan.*

A: Joe DiMaggio of the New York Yankees retired at that figure in 1953. His was the first contract at the magic figure in the history of team sports in this country.

Q: *I had the honor this spring of playing in a pro-am celebrity tournament with Joe DiMaggio, and I realized we don't have sports heroes like him anymore—reserved and dignified and keeping his problems to himself, which is the way I remember DiMaggio as a player. Why is it today's stars are always out front and experts on everything? —Joseph Reynolds, Chicago.*

A: Media pressure is greater than in DiMaggio's day and, what's more, the action is coast-to-coast. But DiMaggio was always essentially the Quiet Man. The classic story on this trait is the time a sportswriter sat in a hotel lobby near DiMaggio and his taciturn friends, Frank Crosetti and Tony Lazzeri, clocking their conversation. After an hour and twenty minutes of silence, DiMaggio cleared his throat. Crosetti said, "What did you say?" and Lazzeri said, "Shut up, he didn't say nothing."

Q: *You mentioned in the "Hot Line" Joe DiMaggio and his hitting streak of 56 games. Rico Carty of the Atlanta Braves had a hitting streak one year near the streak of DiMaggio's. How close did Carty get and in what year did this happen? —Wayne Holzlohner, West Palm Beach.*

A: Carty had a streak of 31 games in 1970. Willie Davis, for the LA Dodgers, also hit in 31 straight in 1973. That's the closest anyone has come since Tommy Holmes set the National League mark of 37 in 1945.

Q: *I have seen references to the phrase "Where have you gone, Joe DiMaggio?" a number of times in the past year. What does it mean and where did it come from? I know Joe is in San Francisco with a fish restaurant. —Carlo D'Antoni, Huntington, Pennsylvania.*

A: The line, which ends, "A nation turns its lonely eyes to you," is from the song "Mrs. Robinson," background music of *The Graduate* film. Here's what lyricist Paul Simon says about the phrase: "My style is to write with free association, and as soon as I said the Joe DiMaggio line I said to myself, 'That's a great line.' It has a nice feeling of nostalgia to it. It has something to do with heroes, people who are all good with no bad in them at all. That's the way I always saw Joe DiMaggio."

Q: *Jim Murray said in a column that Joe DiMaggio would rather drop a fly ball than do something undignified in public. Did Joe ever drop a fly ball? I saw Mickey Mantle do it once. If Joe did, how many times?* —*Charles J. May, Mount Home, Idaho.*

A: On May 30, 1950, in the third inning of the first game of a doubleheader, DiMag dropped a third-out pop fly to short right-center. It must have been a long day for Joe. He was 0–for–6 as the Yankees beat the Red Sox twice. We were able to pinpoint that one, but longtime Yankee watchers say he dropped a couple others early in his career. The DiMaggio legend has grown to such proportions that people tend to forget he was human. His admirers point out that Joe never dropped one in the clutch.

Q: *I enjoy Joe Garagiola on TV. If I remember correctly, he wasn't all that bad as a catcher. Didn't he set a record of some kind in the 1946 World Series?* —*Mason LeBeau, Wichita.*

A: As a rookie catcher, Garagiola hit .316 as the Cardinals won the series from Boston. He collected four hits in one game, the fourth, tying a record held at that time by twenty-five others, including Ty Cobb. He drove in three runs and tagged out a runner at home. Remembers Joe: "I went back to the hotel in Boston and bought a copy of every paper in town. They had about thirty-two of them in Boston in those days. I climbed into bed with the papers, all set to read about my great day. They had headlines six inches tall: WILLIAMS BEATS OUT BUNT. Ted Williams had beaten the Cardinals' infield shift with a bunt single, eclipsing Garagiola's four hits and a 12–3 Cardinal win.

Q: *This phony used to be a sandlot catcher, never could hit, Mr. Nice Guy, a Dodge Boy, on different TV panels. Maybe you know who I am talking about. Well, this character would let a black cat out of a bag onto the field when Jackie Robinson first appeared at Sportsman's Park. Let some of the brothers know who weren't born when it happened. —Paul Ringer, Cincinnati.*

A: When you said "Mr. Nice Guy," we realized you meant Joe Garagiola. The black cat actually leaped out of the bag in Montreal, where Jackie played the year before moving up to Brooklyn, and Joe had nothing to do with it. His only run-in with Robinson came when catcher Garagiola argued with an ump over a strike that was called a ball. Batter Robinson put in an opinion and Garagiola said, "You stay out of this—let him miss all the calls." After a few more heated words, Robinson knocked the dirt out of his spikes and told Garagiola something he says he always remembered: "We don't have to like each other, but we have to work together."

Q: *Every time I see or hear anything about Babe Ruth they bring up the time he said he was having "a better year" than President Hoover. Did he really say something like that, and wasn't that a terribly disrespectful thing to say about a President? —Monte Cooke, Salem, Oregon.*

A: Ruth had just signed an $80,000 contract in 1931 and a reporter said to him, "You're making more money than the President." The Babe replied, "Why not? I had a better year than he did." Though it's typical of these sophisticated times to regard that story as apocryphal, Ruth did say it—and remember that Herbert Hoover was having worse things said about him at the time. Ruth's political background explains the wisecrack. In 1928, Ruth campaigned for fellow Catholic Al Smith, the Democrat opposing Hoover. He even organized a "political action group," Yankees for Smith. When Hoover once visited Yankee Stadium, Ruth stayed in the clubhouse so he wouldn't have to shake the President's hand.

Q: *Whitey Ford broke Babe Ruth's World Series pitching record, Roger Maris "broke" his season-homer total, and now Henry Aaron has broken his career home-run record. Is there anything left for the Babe in the record books? —Charles W., Boise.*

A: Safe from all challengers is Ruth's career total of bases on balls—2,056. Good eye, Babe.

Q: *Can you tell me what Babe Ruth did in his LAST official game? —R.A.R., Chicago.*

A: On May 30, 1935, at Philadelphia, the Babe went hitless in his only time at bat in the first game of a doubleheader, and threw out a runner. He was replaced in left field by Hal Lee, went into the locker room, changed clothes, and left baseball forever. On May 25, he had hit three home runs for the Boston Braves against Pittsburgh. That's often mistakenly remembered as his last game.

Q: *Is it true that when Babe Ruth was playing and a home team won in the ninth or extra innings, a home run didn't count if the winning run scored ahead of it? If so, how many did Ruth hit that didn't count? —G. Mihecoby, Downey, California.*

A: True. Ruth only "lost" one homer this way, during his pitching days with the Boston Red Sox in 1918. You could look it up: July 8.

Q: *Was Babe Ruth ever intentionally walked: with the bases full, a runner on first, first and third, or the bases empty? —Henry M. Mereness, Riviera Beach, Florida.*

A: Ruth was walked purposely in all those situations, a sign of the respect pitchers held for him throughout his home-run career. With the bases full, a Yankee opponent holding less than a four-run lead had the choice of forcing in one run via a walk to the Babe, or risking them all. The first batter ever to receive such tribute, however, was one of great-grandpa's favorites, Napoleon Lajoie, who hit .422 in 1921.

Q: *I need to know Babe Ruth's original name, for a planned article. If you have that information available without a lot of digging, I'll be mighty grateful. —Virgil Hancock, Bellaire, Texas.*

A: Your question indicates you are probably a victim of the once-circulated story that the Babe's name was "originally" either Ehrhardt or Gerhardt. Indeed, he was raised in an orphanage, the St. Mary's Industrial School for Boys, after his parents deemed him "incorrigible" at age eight, namely because he drank liquor, chewed tobacco, and stole anything that wasn't nailed down. But the bottom-line truth is that the Babe was born George Herman Ruth, Jr.

Q: *I have seen more stories about Babe Ruth this year than I have the rest of my life. I saw one mention that he and Ty Cobb were lifelong enemies, but it didn't say why. Did they ever have a fight, or was this just a natural jealousy between two top players? — August Hoting, West Palm Beach.*

A: Their enmity was real and earnest, though they made up in their declining years at a World War II bond rally. It stemmed from Cobb's vicious taunts when trying to unsettle the Babe in games against Detroit. Cobb would yell, "Hey, nigger!" It was once the prevailing rumor in baseball that Ruth had black ancestors. Cobb carried through with this pose even off field, once refusing to share a room with Ruth on a hunting trip. "I've never bedded down with a nigger, and I'm not going to start now," he said.

In Jerry Holtzman's great book, *No Cheering in the Press Box,* the venerable Fred Lieb recalls a Yankees—

Tigers brawl in which Cobb raced in from center field and Ruth came roaring off the bench: "They met like two football linemen, each trying to put the other out of play. One shot out in one direction and the other in the other."

Q: *Pete Axthelm in a* Newsweek *cover story on Nolan Ryan, referred to Dazzy Vance as one of three Brooklyn base runners who once wound up on the same base at the same time. What's the story there?* — *Rody Miller, Gainesville, Florida.*

A: This classic incident of 1926 resulted in a retelling by the late John Lardner, as follows: "The bases were full of Brooklyns, with one out, when Babe Herman strode to the plate. Scattered around the landscape before him were Hank DeBerry on third base, Dazzy Vance on second, and Chick Fewster on first. Mr. Herman swung ferociously and the ball hit the right-field wall on a line. DeBerry scored. Vance hovered between second and third for a moment, on the theory the ball might be caught. When it rebounded off the wall, he set sail again, lumbering to third base, and made a tentative turn toward home. Then, deciding he couldn't score, he stepped back to third. This move confounded Fewster, who was hard on Vance's heels. Fewster started back toward second base. At that moment, a new character with blond hair and flapping ears, came into their lives.

"Mr. Herman ran with blinkers on, as they say at the racetrack. Passing Fewster like the Limited passing a whistle stop, the Babe slid into third just as Vance returned there from the opposite direction. Herman was automatically out for passing Fewster on the base line, though nobody realized it at once except the umpire, who made an 'out' sign.

"The third baseman, not knowing who was out, began frantically to tag Herman, who was already dead, and Vance, who stood perfectly safe on third base.

"The third baseman looked in vain to the umpire
156

for the sign of another out. Fewster, confused, stood a little distance away. His proper move was to go back to second and stay there, but Herman's slide had destroyed his powers of thought. Finally, the third baseman began to chase Fewster, who ran in panic and did not even stop at second, where he would have been safe. He was tagged in the outfield for the third out of the inning."

As Lardner had noted, Babe Herman had tripled into a double play.

Q: *Much has been written about Babe Ruth's homers and Joe DiMaggio's hit streak. Since DiMaggio began fourteen years after Ruth's career ended, I wonder if any pitcher gave up a homer to Ruth and later a hit to DiMaggio? —Colin Nelson, Norwalk, Connecticut.*

A: We would have bet against it, but you're right. There were two, and both are in the Hall of Fame. Ted Lyons of Chicago and Lefty Grove of Philadelphia and Boston. Babe hit Lyons for his 54th and Grove for his 57th on the way to 60 in 1927. DiMaggio hit Grove in game 11 and Lyons in game 52.

Q: *Most of us know that Yankee numbers 3, 4, 5, and 7 were worn by Ruth, Gehrig, DiMaggio, and Mantle. But who wore No. 6? —Fred Cavalos, New Brunswick, New Jersey.*

A: There has been no Big 6 in Yankee history, no certifiable Hall of Famer, that is. Perhaps the most notable Yankee 6 was third baseman, now doctor, Bobby Brown, part owner of the Texas Rangers. The Yankee line continued with a great 8, Yogi Berra.

Q: *At the last Yankees' Old-timers game in Shea Stadium, I found out that seven Yankees had had their numbers retired by the club—Ruth, Gehrig, DiMaggio, Mantle, Berra, Dickey, and Stengel. Are the Yankees the only team in the American League to do this? It's a nice honor and there must be other greats who deserve such an honor.* —*Karl Solomon, Lansing, Michigan.*

A: Only four non-Yankees have had their numbers retired by their old American League teams—Bob Feller (19) and Lou Boudreau (5) by Cleveland, Ted Williams (9) by Boston, and Frank Robinson (20) by Baltimore. Obviously, Robinson's the only player in the American League whose number was retired before he was.

Q: *Now Cool Papa Bell is in the Baseball Hall of Fame along with Josh Gibson and Satchel Paige and others, I have often wondered, with all these great players available, why was Jackie Robinson picked to break the color line? —Herman Klein, Cincinnati.*

A: Robinson was judged to have the correct blend of education, courage, and talent—with most of his career still in front of him. Branch Rickey, Jackie's great patron, once apologized to Satchel Paige, assuring him, "If I'd had my way, you would have been the first." Rickey didn't elaborate, and Paige was asked to explain what this meant. Said Satchel: "Mr. Rickey, as the Bible says, sometimes spake in diverse tongues."

Q: *Satchel Paige gave great advice when he said not to look back, somebody might be gaining on you. But I remember that he had a whole list of things like that. Would you look it up for me? —Larry G., Sacramento.*

A: Satchel had six. Here are the first five: Avoid fried meats which angry up the blood. If your stomach disputes you, lie down and pacify it with cool thoughts. Keep the juices moving by jangling around gently as you walk. Go light on the vices such as carrying on in society. Avoid running at all times.

Q: *Jimmy Wynn was a big star with the Dodgers after being a disappointment—a flop?—at Houston. Does he have an explanation for this, and what do other baseball people say? —Conrad Dieterle, San Diego.*

A: Wynn says only, "There's magic in the Dodger

uniform." Insiders point out that 1974 was the first season since 1967 that Wynn had been free of both injury and domestic travail. The latter reached a climax when he was stabbed by his wife in a post-midnight argument after celebrating their wedding anniversary. Wynn is now remarried.

Q: *Hank Aaron got all the ink, but isn't Nolan Ryan's strikeout record going to last a long time, too? —Horace W., St. Louis.*

A: Leave Henry out of this. But Ryan's 383 total is likely to last forever if the National League goes to the designated hitter. Sandy Koufax's 382 total included strikeouts of 52 pitchers. Not one hurler is in Ryan's figure. However, Ryan's greatest achievement was marrying the 1958 Hula Hoop champion of Alvin, Texas, his own baby Ruth.

Q: *On the "Game of the Week," I heard Curt Gowdy say that neither Nolan Ryan nor Sandy Koufax was the fastest pitcher he ever saw. He said Herb Score, the old Cleveland left-hander, was the fastest, at least before his eye injury. And Tony Kubek agreed. A few days later, several American League players, including Reggie Jackson, were quoted as saying they feared for their lives when they faced Ryan. Now, my question is, which pitcher was the most feared in the years since the war? Ryan, Koufax, Feller, or Score? —Leonard Patek, Austin.*

A: Since there are no surveys on the subject, you can take your choice. But a pretty good candidate would be Ryne Duren, the onetime Yankee relief pitcher and wildman, who wore eyeglasses as thick as Coke bottles and whose wildness was legendary. When Duren warmed up in the bullpen, it sounded like a cannon going off. When he loosened up on the mound, he consistently threw his first pitch against the backstop. Once, Duren walked three straight hitters on twelve pitches, forcing in a run. He stormed up to the home-plate umpire and demanded, "Where the (bleep) are those pitches?" The umpire raised his hand to his chin. "Well," fumed Duren, "I've got to have that pitch."

Q: *I have a Little Leaguer who copies everything Pete Rose does, and that's the problem. Why does Pete always seem to slide headfirst into a base? That may come under the heading of "hustling," but it isn't the way the coaches teach it. And how does Pete keep from getting hurt? —Glenn Stowers, Norfolk, Virginia.*

A: Pete Rose doesn't recommend his base-sliding style to youngsters, but on the other hand he doesn't agree that it is riskier than the conventional way. "You can break your ankle or your legs a lot faster," he says, "than you can your belly or your arm." The second reason Pete slides headfirst is that when you do "You usually get your picture in the paper."

Q: *Who is the former head of the CIA who had a job in sports as the secretary to Branch Rickey with the St. Louis Browns in 1915? —Wm. O. DeWitt, Cincinnati.*

A: Letter-writer Bill DeWitt, one-time owner of the St. Louis Browns and the Cincinnati Reds, is obviously testing Hot Line's capabilities for an answer he already knows: The young law student who worked for Rickey, then business manager of the Browns, later became Rear Admiral Roscoe H. Hillenkoetter, USN, who was the first director of the CIA.

Q: *Looking through the* Encyclopedia of Baseball, *I noticed that Happy Chandler was the only commissioner whose name wasn't mentioned. Can you tell me why this is? Also, is he still living? —Harvey Seidman, St. Louis.*

A: According to the publisher, it was an editorial oversight, as opposed to a historical one. But the place of Happy Chandler in baseball has long been a curious one. The old guard among the owners never forgave him for defying them on certain key issues, and when

Chandler's contract was not renewed in 1951, independence was not a trait they sought in future candidates. But today some baseball historians are rethinking Happy's role, and a move is afoot to elect him to the Hall of Fame. During his five years in office, the color line was broken, the television age began, and Leo Durocher was suspended for a full season for consorting with "questionable" characters. When the owners voted 15-to-1 AGAINST admitting blacks into the majors, Chandler overruled them and supported Branch Rickey's decision to bring up Jackie Robinson. At seventy-six, the onetime Kentucky Senator is still practicing law, in Versailles, and remains a force in the state's Democratic party.

Q: *Has there ever been a left-handed catcher? If so, who was the last one?* —*Randy Zeck, Mason City, Illinois.*

A: Dale Long caught in two games in 1958 for the Chicago Cubs, the result of an earlier experiment of Branch Rickey's, when Long was with Pittsburgh. Rickey gave up on the idea because lefties don't throw a straight ball. That's why they call them "crooked arms." The last full-time lefty catcher, Jack Clements, retired in 1900 after 1,100 games.

Q: *Awhile back somebody asked about gamblers trying to fix games by getting to the officials. I know there was a case several years ago in baseball and I think the umpires involved blew the whistle. It seems to me it all came out during the World Series one year. Is there any way to check this?* —*Doug Brocato, Detroit.*

A: The incident occurred late in the season of 1960 in Baltimore, where two umpires, Ed Runge and Bill McKinley, made the mistake of letting themselves be picked up by two young ladies in a bar. Hours later, a pair of ex-convicts threatened to blackmail them with damaging photographs, unless the umpires agreed to buy the negatives for $5,000 or to fix a game, or games, on which the blackmailers would bet. In an act of some courage, Runge and McKinley reported the attempt both to the American League and the Maryland police. By fighting back and going public, the umpires turned a moment of folly into a plus for the integrity of sports.

Q: *I sit behind the plate at Red Sox games and my question is: Don't the umpires have to have 20-20 vision to work in the majors? —Charles M., Boston.*

A: They are tested periodically, but uncorrected 20-20 is not required. Umpires would never admit to having less than perfect vision until Ed Rommel broke tradition by wearing specs on the ball field in 1956.

Q: *How many sets of three or more brothers have made it to the major leagues? —Louise Smith, Oroville, California.*

A: In modern times, there were the DiMaggios—Dom, Vince, and Joe; the Alous—Felipe, Matty, and Jesus; and the Boyers—Ken, Clete, and Cloyd.

Q: *The baseball movie,* Bang the Drum Slowly, *is about a pitcher and a catcher, and the catcher is dying of Hodgkin's disease. An old-timer friend of mine says the story is taken from real life, that the catcher was with Cincinnati and he killed himself. If so, what was the guy's name and what was the pitcher's name? —Richard K., Pittsburgh.*

A: Your old-timer's memory is fair but scrambled. Willard Hershberger was a back-up catcher for pennant-winning Cincinnati when he slashed his wrists in a hotel bathtub. The only pitcher who connects up is Hugh Casey, of the Dodgers, who years later took his life with a shotgun. Hershberger's death remains a mystery. Author Mark Harris did not devise his fine novel around either Hershberger or Casey.

Q: *There's supposed to be a player who wore the name of his hometown on the back of his uniform. In the major leagues. I can't believe this because it's only*

162

in the last few years they've been wearing their names.
—Horace Cook, Des Moines.

A: This is a trivia oddity making the rounds. The player was Bill Voiselle of the New York Giants and his hometown was Ninety-Six, North Carolina.

Q: *Did Willie Mays ever win the RBI championship? —Philmore Phillips, S.S. President Jefferson, Panama Canal Zone.*

Q: *Willie Mays retired in 1973 at a $125,000 salary. I'm curious. How much did he get when he signed with the Giants? —Nate F., Miami.*

A: The sailor's question first: Mays, at one time or another in his twenty-two year career, led the league in batting average, home runs, triples, runs, hits, stolen bases, and bases on balls. But never in runs batted in. Mays had been discovered as a fifteen-year-old by the then Boston Braves. When the Giants signed him four years later for a $10,000 bonus, Braves owner Lou Perini wanted to know how he got away. His head scout explained, "I had two men watching Mays and both agreed he was not worth a penny over $7,500." That's why Mays and Hank Aaron didn't become teammates.

Q: *Joe E. Brown died in 1973. Didn't he make a series of baseball pictures years ago? I can't remember the names or much else, but I know he did. —Alan Summers, Portland, Oregon.*

A: Joe E., father of Pittsburgh G.M. Joe Brown, once had a player's contract in Organized Baseball, but gave it up to play vaudeville. He is best remembered as the star of Ring Lardner's *Alibi Ike,* but he also made other baseball films, including one based on pitcher Rube Waddell's exploits, entitled *Fireman, Save My Child!* Waddell, while with the Philly A's, would leave the bull pen to chase fire trucks.

Q: *Gamblers know that the easiest way to fix a sports event is to bribe the officials or referees. My question is, has there ever been an umpire known to be guilty of aiding a fix? —Larry Porter, Fort Wayne.*

A: Not in Organized Baseball. Aside from the credible honesty of the umpires, there is a natural reason for this. Big money bettors would never put up the house and lot on a game where they had the home-plate ump in their pocket. They believe he could influence a game importantly, but not surely. However in 1972, when state police raided a suburban Baltimore bookmaker, they found the names and addresses and telephone numbers of eleven American League umpires. Commissioner Bowie Kuhn met with the state attorney and nothing has been heard of the case since.

Q: *In the obituaries about Bud Abbott it seems the thing he was most famous for with Costello was the "Who's on first?" skit they did. I have been unable to find a copy of this anywhere. I know Who's on first and What is the name of the guy on second, but who were the other players in the lineup? —August Towne, Dayton.*

A: I Don't Know on third, Tomorrow's the pitcher, Today is the catcher, and I Don't Give a Darn is at short. The *First Fireside Book of Baseball* (Simon & Schuster), edited by Charles Einstein, has the routine verbatim.

Q: *I have been a St. Louis Cardinal fan since the "Gas House Gang." Can you tell me who gave them this name and who were the actual players? —John F. DeGeorge, North Tarrytown, New York.*

A: The St. Louis team in 1935 had played a Saturday doubleheader in Boston and couldn't get their uniforms cleaned before they had to catch a train to New York. When they trooped onto the Polo Grounds next day in their crummy apparel, sportwriters Frank Graham and Bill Corum began talking about "kids from the other side of the tracks," where the gasworks were. Their stories the next day included the phrase "Gas House Gang." The Cardinal style of play fitted this description, with Pepper Martin sliding headfirst into every base, and Leo Durocher spitting on the umpires' shoes. The label was retroactively credited to the World Champion team of 1934, but these were the other major players: Player-manager Frankie Frisch, Dizzy Dean, Rip Collins, Joe Medwick, Wild Bill Hallahan, Bill DeLancey, and Ernie Orsatti.

Q: *Could you please send me the names of the 1927 Yankees known as "Murderers' Row?"* —*Marty Rossman, Skokie, Illinois.*

A: You mean Tony Lazzeri, Lou Gehrig, Babe Ruth, Earle Combs, and Bob Meusel—but they weren't the original Murderers' Row. The originals on the Yankees pre-dated Ruth's arrival when a newspaper cartoonist in 1919 hung the tag on Ping Bodie, Roger Peckinpaugh, Duffy Lewis, and Home Run Baker. For more on Baker, read on.

Q:*In all the stories about home runs lately, I was amazed to see that Home Run Baker, a great name, only hit nine when he led the league one year. Did that earn him the name, and what was his real name?* —*Bert Griffin, Albany, New York.*

A: John Franklin Baker, a third baseman, won his sobriquet in the 1911 World Series when he hit a high fast ball off the Giants' Rube Marquard, and Christy Mathewson made headlines by saying, "So what, the guy can't hit a low curve." Whereupon Baker hit a Mathewson low curve over the right-field fence next day and became Home Run forever. Two home runs in two games in those days was equivalent to Johnny Vander Meer's back-to-back no-hitters years later. At the time, Baker was a member of the Philly A's "100,000 infield," but that's another story.

Q: *I know Ruth was great, but I am tired of reading about the 1927 Yankees being kings of the home run. When I grew up in the late 30s the Yankees practically owned the home run. Didn't one of those teams hit*

more homers than Ruth's bunch? —Eddie Demere-
eaux, Norfolk, Virginia.

A: The perfect glorification for the great Yankee
hitters of that era is the phrase "Five O'Clock Lightning." When King Kong Keller, Joe Gordon, Tommy
Henrich, Joe DiMaggio, and Bill Dickey (not necessarily in that order) came to bat in the seventh and
eighth innings, the lightning was blinding at about 5
o'clock eastern standard time. Those Yankee teams
twice hit a high 174 homers, compared to 1927's total
of 158. The Maris-Mantle Yankees of 1961, however,
hold the current team homer record, 240, but the
sportswriters of their era had run out of inspiration
—except for "the M&M Boys."

Q: *My boy is eight years old and I am undecided*
about starting him up the Little League ladder. Can
you tell me how professional players feel about this
subject? —Troy Ingram, Bethlehem, Pennsylvania.

A: The consensus among major leaguers is that the
Little League is okay as long as it is low pressure and
the accent is on the fun of the game. They abhor
overcoaching and the attitude "winning is the only
thing." Houston third baseman Doug Rader recalls his
own Little League days in Illinois: "We had a little
park across the road from a tavern. My dad and four
or five others would dump all the equipment and say,
'Okay, you boys get together and choose up teams and
play.' Then they'd go across the street and have a
couple beers and let us play. It was different for the
games, but we learned by participating. That's how we
practiced."

Q: *Who holds the baseball record for stealing home*
in a game and a season? —Ricky Wesson, St. Louis.

A: Ty Cobb holds the lifetime mark with 34. Pete
Reiser of Brooklyn (1946) and Rod Carew of Minnesota (1969) share the season record, seven. The
one-game record is two, held by Cobb, Vic Power of

Cleveland, Shoeless Joe Jackson, and five others. But not Jackie Robinson.

Q: *Beer gets the blame for riots at baseball games, but beer is part of baseball. Surely some of the thinkers in the game are working out a way to keep the beer and stop the rowdies. If they are, I'd like to know about it. —Joe Regan, Philadelphia.*

A: The trouble with promoting ten-cent beer nights is that they attract beer drinkers who care nothing about baseball. The solution is simple—announce ten-cent beer AFTER the fans are in the park. Ironically, one of baseball's most embarrassing moments resulted from a ban on beer. At the 1931 World Series in Philadelphia the crowd alternated in booing President Herbert Hoover and chanting, "We want beer!" It was during Prohibition and Hoover was on the side of the drys. It is the only time a President has been booed at a baseball park.

Q: *Have there been any no-hit games where the pitcher has lost? I don't mean like Wayne Garland got beat in the ninth by Oakland. I mean no-hitter all the way. —Butch Peterson, Granite City, Illinois.*

A: Several pitchers (Harvey Haddix, Jim Maloney, Bobo Newsom) have had no-hitters through nine and then lost on extra-inning hits, but only one has done what you described. On April 23, 1964, Ken Johnson, of the then Houston Colt .45s, pitched a no-hit game and lost 1-0 to Cincinnati when he threw wild on a play at first base.

Q: *Baseball and football are talking expansion again. I know the Mets won the World Series, but overall how have the other expansion teams done? —Ken Overmire, Rutherford, New Jersey.*

A: None of the other seven expansion teams has ever won a division title and only one, Houston, has ever finished second. By contrast, two NFL teams (Dallas, Miami) have won the Super Bowl, which seems

167

to prove that pro football's mechanics are better equalizers than baseball's.

Q: *Many years ago the Detroit Tigers had a real "beauty" of a pitcher named Boots Poffenberger. Most people don't believe me. Please put him on record for me.* —Marty Byle, Grand Rapids.

A: Cletus Elwood (Boots) Poffenberger was one of the famous drinkers and night walkers of baseball legend. A great minor league star (Southern Association), Boots won 16 and lost 12 in three seasons with Detroit while setting various records off the field. He was finally fired by Brooklyn manager Leo Durocher in 1939 for jumping the NY-Boston Train. Boots was thoughtful enough to leave a dummy in his berth so Lippy would have someone to talk to at bed-check. He drifted back to the minors until 1943 when he joined the Marines.

Q: *Would you please print some information about Pete Gray, the one-armed outfielder with the old St. Louis Browns? I cannot find anything about him in any of my sports books.* —Charles Young, Mount Home, Idaho.

A: The saddest line in *The Baseball Encyclopedia* is "Pete Gray, 6-1, 169 pounds, bats left, throws left." Gray played 77 games as an outfielder for the Browns in 1945, when they finished third, batted .218. He had been a .300 hitter in the Southern Association. Gray would catch the ball, tuck his glove under the stump of his right arm, grab the ball as it rolled out, and throw. He was skinny, fleet of foot, stole five bases for the Browns. He lost his arm in a childhood accident.

Q: *Can you explain how arbitration works in baseball? Are there any fixed rules or factors that determine whether or not the player gets the salary he wants?* —Byron Sibley, St. Louis.

A: Under the plan adopted in 1973, a player dissatisfied with his team's contract offer can submit the dispute to an arbitrator assigned by the Labor Relations Board. The figures then filed by the player and the team do not necessarily have to be the last submitted by either side. At that point it becomes not unlike a game of bluff poker. The final verdict is purely a judgment call by the arbitrator, who can accept the player's figure or the team's, but no compromise.

The uncertainty of the system is reflected in the 1974 case of outfielder Norm Miller, then with Atlanta. Although appearing in fewer than ten games due to a back injury, Miller sought a raise of $5,000 to $35,000 —and won. In spring training he found himself nearly as big a celebrity as Hank Aaron, who was closing in on Babe Ruth. "The writers all went to Aaron," said Miller proudly, "but the other players came to me."

Q: *Surely Gaylord and Jim Perry of Cleveland must be the greatest pitching brothers of all time. Can you tell me what brothers are second, and what are the totals? —Sam Whittington, San Diego.*

A: The Perry Brothers had 409 wins going into this season. The question of second place is tricky. Officially it's the Mathewsons with 373, all of which were won by Christy. Harry Mathewson pitched several times for the Giants but never got a victory. Behind them come Stanley and Harry Coveleski, 297; Jesse and Virgil Barnes, 213; and Dizzy and Daffy Dean, 200.

Q: *I lived near Yankee Stadium when Billy Martin broke in with the club. A bunch of us kids used to hang around the box seats during batting practice, until the ushers chased us away, and I remember clearly that Martin was not popular. The veterans used to needle him and ride him, and opposing players had a nickname for him I can't recall. Does Billy admit to this, and can you find out what his nickname was? —Henry Margolin, West Newton, Massachusetts.*

A: The Yankees treated Martin as they did all newcomers—unmercifully. But Billy gave it right back. "Some couldn't take it so good, either," he says. "After a while they left me alone." The bench jockeys of that time called him "Barrymore," in honor of the nose he had remodeled. The Yankees came to accept Martin and later to follow him, but he never did fit the mold. Now there is a new Yankee image, and the peripatetic Billy Martin is the manager.

Q: *Can you tell me about Ron LeFlore, the player the Detroit Tigers signed out of prison? What did he do, and how did they find him? —Manny Gilbert, Little Rock.*

A: At seventeen, LeFlore and two buddies held up a small store in a Detroit neighborhood, cleaning out the register and dumping the money in a brown paper bag. They were arrested before they could even count it. A first offender, LeFlore was given a sentence of five-to-fifteen years. He was nearing parole when the Tigers sent out a goodwill party, headed by then manager Billy Martin, to the Southern Michigan State Prison. There the inmates harangued Martin until a tryout was arranged for LeFlore, the prison's star athlete. A football halfback, he was scouted by ex-pro Dick (Night Train) Lane, on behalf of Wilberforce College. Now LeFlore is a big league centerfielder, with no high school experience, less than a season in the minors, and three years of prison behind him.

Q: *I am familiar with the famous baseball poem by Franklin P. Adams that celebrated the deeds of Tinker, Evers, and Chance. What I can't seem to find out is how many double plays this combination recorded. Can you get this information for me? —Chris Provost, Little Rock.*

A: "These are the saddest of possible words, Tinker-to-Evers-to-Chance." So goes the opening line of Adams' poem, "Baseball's Sad Lexicon." Exactly what inspired Adams isn't known, but the sad truth is the immortal Chicago Cubs' trio accounted for a total of only 54 double plays in four seasons.

Q: *Can you tell me the origin of the baseball phrase "Good field, no hit"? —John Urquardt, Dayton.*

A: Way back in 1924, when Moe Berg was a fledgling shortstop in the Brooklyn chain, the Minneapolis club wanted to buy his contract during spring training. Mike Kelley sent a telegram to Miguel Gonzales, then a coach with St. Louis, asking for an evaluation of Berg. Gonzales sent back his famous four-word reply. Berg became a catcher, and though Gonzales' estimate proved correct over the long haul (a .243 lifetime average), he did hit .287 for the White Sox in 1929, as a catcher.

Still later, Berg engaged in atomic espionage in Europe during World War II and worked for the CIA afterward. A linguist of genius stature, Berg could read and write Sanskrit as well as seventeen other languages. Casey Stengel called him "the strangest fellah I ever met."

Q: *I have lost track of Bo Belinsky, the kookie left-hander who once pitched for the Los Angeles Angels. Is he married? Where is he and what does he do for a living, if anything? —Anthony Urbanik, San Bernardino, California.*

A: Bo Baby, who also made stops in Philadelphia, Houston, and Chicago during his big league odyssey, has settled in his favorite playground, Hawaii. In 1973, according to Belinsky, he was on the verge of becoming an alcoholic. He has since acquired a new life-style, a new moustache, and a new bride, the former Jane Weyerhaeuser, the lumber heiress. The Belinskys are now pricing Thoroughbred horses. Bo is still in there, pitching.

Q: *Al Kaline never played in the minors and he spent his entire career with the Detroit Tigers. Have any others done this? If so, who? —Mrs. Vicky Page, East Detroit, Michigan.*

A: Kaline shares that distinction with several others, most notably Mel Ott (New York Giants), Sandy

Koufax (Dodgers), and Bob Feller (Cleveland). A footnote is required in the case of Feller, whose contract was assigned in 1936 to Fargo-Moorehead in the Northern League. He refused to report. His contract was sold to New Orleans. He refused to report. Whereupon the Indians gave up, brought him to Cleveland, and launched his record-breaking career.

Q: *A close friend of mine, dead about twenty-two years, told me many times the following sports trivia which has plagued me: Is it true or false that Floyd Giebell pitched only once in the majors as he and Detroit knocked Bobby Feller and Cleveland out of the American League pennant in 1940—Cleveland folding, as usual, in the clutch? —Art Kehoe, Jr., Rutherford, New Jersey.*

A: This is another sample of baseball's mythology. Floyd Giebell was a thirty-year-old rookie who pitched briefly for the Tigers in 1939 (one win, one loss) and had his moment in the sun the next year. Two days before the end of the 1940 season, Giebell, chosen because Manager Bucky Harris didn't want to waste an ace against 27-game winner Feller, pitched a six-hit shutout as the Tigers won, 2-0, clinching the pennant. It was the last game he ever won in the majors, though he appeared in seventeen box scores in 1941, mostly in relief, with no decisions.

Q: *I got a laugh out of the charges that Don Sutton of the Dodgers doctors his pitches with sandpaper. Don't all pitchers cheat? As I recall, they used to frisk Don Drysdale during almost every game. Did they ever prove anything on him? —Vernon McCamey, Dayton.*

A: A former Dodger coach, Preston Gomez, says Drysdale used a surgical jelly while setting a major league record in 1968 of 58 and ⅔ scoreless innings. "He kept the stuff in a different spot every inning," reveals Gomez. "His hat, his glove, all over his body. One game during the streak the other team accused Drysdale of putting grease on the ball and the umpire walked to the mound to check. Drysdale took off his hat, swept it through the air to show the crowd, and ran his hand all through his hair to prove he had no grease on his head. He had it in his belt that night."

According to an informal survey once conducted by Jim Bouton, of "Ball Four" fame, not ALL pitchers cheat. Only 87 percent.

Q: *In all the stories I have read about baseball's Black Sox scandal, a couple of things have never been clear to me. Was the case broken by the police, or by baseball? And did any of the players involved in the fix go to jail?* —Arnold Sapinsky, Daytona Beach.

A: The case actually began to unravel when pitcher Eddie Cicotte, guilt-ridden over his part in having rigged, or attempted to rig, the 1919 World Series, confessed to Charles Comiskey, owner of the Chicago White Sox. Cicotte was urged to do this by his priest. Then one of the game's best pitchers, he started three times against the Reds, lost twice. It was a full year before Cicotte blew the whistle. Eight players stood trial, all took the Fifth Amendment and were acquitted for lack of evidence. Judge Kenesaw Mountain Landis barred them from baseball for life.

Q: *Several professional athletes have been married to or linked with glamour girls and movie starlets during their playing careers. Examples include Marilyn Monroe and Joe DiMaggio, Bo Belinsky and Jo Collins; former Major Leaguer Don Rudolph was married to stripper Patti Waggin. I've heard that National League umpire Dick Stello also is married to an exotic dancer who also had a couple of roles in films. Is he married to Chesty Morgan, the exotic with the seventy-three-inch bust, who recently completed a role in "Double Agent 73"?* —Gary Lee, Indianapolis.

A: Stello is in the third year of marriage (his first) to Miss Morgan, and they live in the off-season at St. Petersburg, Florida. Stello has always been enamored of show biz and used to spend his winters working as an MC for nightclubs in New York and New Jersey. When introduced to Chesty, Stello's famous first-words were: "My, my, seventy-three inches—why that's over six feet!"

Q: *I saw an ex-baseball player on Johnny Carson last night who said something hilarious about Vince Lombardi's "winning is everything." Can you tell me the whole line? —Eddie Gehraty, Passaic, New Jersey.*

A: Bob Uecker, former major league catcher who always threatened to hit .200, is a unique wit on the sports scene, calls games for the Milwaukee Brewers, and is in great demand on the winter banquet circuit. We think you're talking about this Uecker gem: "Winning and losing is nothing. Going out and prowling the streets after the game is what I liked. You'd get half in the bag and wake up the next morning with a bird in your room—that's what baseball is all about."

Q: *When Gates Brown retired from the Detroit Tigers, the stories mentioned that he had served time. I know about Ron LeFlore. But can you tell me about Brown's problem, and how the Tigers got him? — Ernie Gallela, Allentown, Pennsylvania.*

A: The son of a railroad worker, Brown dropped out of school in his senior year in Ohio and then landed in big trouble. He was sentenced to prison for a term of one-to-five years for breaking and entering; he served twenty-one months and walked out into the world with a bonus contract of $7,000.

That was in 1960. Brown was twenty-one, and the Tigers were one of several teams contacted by a prison guard on his behalf. He moved up to Detroit in the middle of the 1963 season, hit a pinch homer in his first time at bat, and went on to become Detroit's all-time pinch hitter. "There's no way I wasn't going to make it," said Gates. "I had to make it. The things that happened to me I asked for. Not many people get a second chance."

Q: *I know that Bill Wambsganss, the old Cleveland second baseman, made the only unassisted triple play in World Series history in 1920. But is it possible to find out who was the player who hit into it?* —*Len Schiller, Roanoke, Virginia.*

A: The luckless batter was Brooklyn pitcher Clarence Mitchell who coincidentally was one of the last honest spitball throwers. While Wamby became immortal, few remember Clarence Mitchell. Ironically, on his next time up, Mitchell hit into a double play, for five outs in two at bat.

Q: *I have a rather ancient question to ask. I have asked it many times before but never got a satisfactory answer. I believe it was in the World Series in baseball between the Cleveland and Brooklyn teams in 1920 that an outfielder, Wambsganss, executed an unassisted triple play. HOW DID HE DO IT?* —*Erik Flamer, Long Beach, California.*

A: Brooklyn's at bat, Pete Kilduff on second and Otto Miller on first, pitcher Clarence Mitchell at the plate. The hit and run is on. Mitchell smashes a line drive over second. Second baseman Billy Wambsganss spears the ball, steps on second, then walks over and tags Miller, who was too stunned to move. Triple play. Cleveland won the game, 8-1, and the Series, five games to two. Brooklyn didn't get into another Series until 1941.

Q: *I have been following sports all my life, but I never thought of this until my kid asked me—why is a left-hander called a "southpaw"?* —*Andy Klinger, Cincinnati.*

A: H. L. Mencken, in his monumental work, *The American Language*, credits Dr. Edward Nichols, of Penn State, with tracking down the origin of the term. Nichols found that Charles Seymour used it in an 1891 edition of the Chicago *Herald*. The city's west side ball park had the pitcher facing into the sun, so his left hand was the south paw. In fact, most baseball parks are oriented so a setting sun won't be in the batter's eyes.

Q: *Has there ever been a switch pitcher in professional baseball?* —*C. A. VanderWerf, Dean, University of Florida, Gainesville.*

A: Baseball historians recall two pitchers who were ambidextrous: Ed Head, with the Brooklyn Dodgers, and Dave (Boo) Ferriss, of the Red Sox, both of whom had their peak years in the 40s. There is no record of a pitcher actually throwing from both sides in the same game; at least, not during the regular season. Ferriss, a free spirit, did it once in a spring exhibition against the Boston Braves. Unlike switch hitters, a pitcher has the problem of changing gloves.

Q: *It is my recollection that the New York Yankees once had three catchers who all hit more than twenty home runs in the same season. Two of the three were Yogi Berra and Elston Howard, but I don't know who the third man was, or the year. Has this ever happened before or since?* —*Charles F. Quigley, Salt Lake City.*

A: The other catcher was John Blanchard and the year was 1961, Ralph Houk's first as a Yankee manager. No other team has had three such productive players alternating behind the plate.

Q: *I've got a bet going that there was one guy who played in the Rose Bowl who also played in a World Series, but now I can't remember his name.* —*E.K.L., Terre Haute.*

A: Neither could we until we looked it up. Then we found two: outfielder Chuck Essegian, who hit the first pinch homer in World Series history for the Dodgers in 1959, and played halfback for UCLA in 1956; and golden boy Jackie Jensen, who qualified with California in 1949 and the Yankees a year later.

Q: *Who was the first man to do play-by-play of a World Series over the radio? If you can answer this, I suppose you can also tell me when it was. —Edward Durbin, Fort Wayne.*

A: Harold Arlin broadcast the 1921 Series over KDKA, a Pittsburgh station, though it was an all-New York battle, Yankees vs. Giants.

Q: *In going through* The Baseball Encyclopedia *I somehow noticed that Lou Gehrig's figures for 1938 list 157 games. But the standings show that his team, the Yankees, only played 152 games. How could this be? —Robert Wimbeley, Hutchinson, Kansas.*

A: Tie games. They count in the player's record, but don't show in the standings. The Yankees played five that year.

Q: *I have been a fan of Reggie Jackson ever since he came to the big leagues. Each year I hear that he has a good chance to win baseball's triple crown. What is the triple crown and who was the last to win it? —Jim Bradford, Clifton, New Jersey.*

A: The answer isn't Secretariat. Baseball's three jewels are: batting average, homers, and runs batted in. The last player to lead in all three categories was Carl Yastrzemski, of Boston, in 1967, hitting .326 with 44 homers and 121 RBI. Yaz is the only triple-crown winner since baseball expanded in 1961.

The last National League batter to turn the trick was Chuck Klein, of the Phillies, in 1933 (.368, 28, 120). Only two other players have achieved that distinction since the war, Ted Williams in 1947 and Mickey Mantle in 1956.

Q: *The way I hear it, Reggie Jackson was at the center of dissension on the Oakland A's. He is probably the biggest star in baseball today, so is his trouble the Big Head, or is it racial? —Cotton Rollins, Fort Lauderdale.*

A: Jackson is an extremely well-adjusted, carefree superstar with many good qualities, such as charitable work and the ability to make money as an investor.

177

His problem with some of his A's teammates was racial, but not as you think. His black brothers think he trucks with whites too much.

Jackson, whose grandmother was Spanish, explains: "My father didn't and still doesn't know what color is. I grew up with white kids [near Philadelphia], played ball with them, went home with them. I didn't know what prejudice was until I got to Arizona State and the football coach told me to stop dating white girls."

Jackson, divorced from his Mexican-American wife, dates several white girls now. "There are 200 million people in this country," he says, "and 180 million of them are white. It's only natural most of my friends are white."

Q: *To me the Oakland A's are the biggest cry-babies in sport. The more they knock Charley Finley, the more I think he must be okay. They made fun of his uniforms, now a lot of teams have copied them. A lot of his other ideas have caught on, like the designated hitter and night World Series games. If the players take his money, why can't they give him some loyalty?*
—Edward Laurent, Baltimore.

A: Your question was put to Sal Bando, the former Oakland captain who was described by Finley—during contract talks—as the eleventh best third baseman in the American League. "The big thing," said Bando, "is his lack of respect for other people. I said last winter that the front office was a one-man show, and he used this as an excuse to call me in and demean me. To me, this is like a car dealer buying time on TV and saying he has the worst cars in town. No wonder people don't come to see us play."

Q: *Every time I read about another old black base-ball player being included in the Hall of Fame, it boils my blood. I don't know how my brothers feel, but I'd just as soon that Satchel Paige and Josh Gibson and Cool Papa Bell told them to take the honor and shove* it, like Bill Russell did. Haven't any of the old black players refused the people who kept them out of the game when it mattered? —Ellis Wallace, Chicago.

A: As far as we know, no. The difference here is the players loved the game of baseball so much they can overlook the oafs who ruled it way back then.

This is what the great Buck Leonard had to say on the subject: "I was in Cooperstown the day Satchel Paige was inducted, and I stayed awake almost all that night thinking about it. It's something you never had any dream you'd ever see. Like men walking on the moon. I always wanted to go up there to Cooperstown. You felt like you had a reason, because it's the home of baseball, but you didn't have a special reason. We never thought we'd get in the Hall of Fame. We thought the way we were playing was the way it was going to continue. I never had any dream it would come. But that night I felt like I was part of it at last."

Q: *Recently the question came up on a Voice of the People program, "How and where did the custom of playing the National Anthem before sporting events originate?" If you know, your help will be appreciated.* —Hollis Francis, WJAG, Norfolk, Nebraska.

A: In the opening game of the 1918 World Series, Boston at Chicago, as the fans stood for the seventh inning stretch, the band suddenly played "The Star-Spangled Banner." The crowd spontaneously began to sing along. This was repeated the following two games in Chicago, and thereafter it was played on opening day, for World Series games, and on special occasions when a band was present. But it didn't become a general practice until the 1942 baseball season as part of the patriotic fervor of World War II. You must also bear in mind that "The Star-Spangled Banner" did not become the official national anthem until Congress adopted it in March, 1931.

Q: *When the old TV program "$64,000 Question" was going, a grandma won the money by answering* *baseball questions. I can't remember her name and I wonder what the final question was?* —*Ellis Ditmer, Norfolk, Virginia.*

A: Myrtle Power was the grandma's name, but she stopped at $32,000 by naming the six players besides Ty Cobb who had more than 3,000 major league hits: Cap Anson, Honus Wagner, Nap Lajoie, Tris Speaker, Eddie Collins, and Paul Waner. If a grandma had to handle that one today, she'd have to add Stan Musial, Robert Clemente, Willie Mays, Hank Aaron, and Al Kaline.

Q: *Peter Marshall, M.C. of "Hollywood Squares," often refers to his son who plays professional baseball. Can you tell us, please, who this son is and where he has played?* —*Mrs. Pat Suba, Galena Park, Texas.*

A: Marshall's son is Ralph Peter LaCock, Jr., a pitcher who broke in with the Chicago Cubs at the end of the 1973 season. Incidentally, it was the father who changed names.

Q: *I am collecting quotes and anecdotes about Mark Fidrych, the rookie Detroit pitcher, because I think he is going to be the greatest personality (and talent) since Dizzy Dean. Would you furnish some material for me?* —*Eddie Campbell, St. Louis.*

A: Fidrych has already been worth a million dollars to baseball in goodwill, as in the way he shook off his loss in the 1976 All Star game: "It was neat being out there. An honor. All my friends got to see me. No one should smile after a loss, but this is different. I can go home proud. And whoever thought I'd meet the President?"

Fidrych stamped himself as something different when he described his reaction in the spring, at Lakeland, Florida, on learning he had made the big club: "I celebrated the way every young fellow would. I climbed the flagpole at the ball park with my girlfriend, slid down the other side, and made love on the mound."

Q: *Don't you agree that Doug Rader's reputation as a clown or a kook has kept him from recognition he deserves as a ballplayer? He has produced a lot of laughs, but you can't cash those at the supermarket. —Hal Livingston, Detroit.*

A: Rader, who won five Gold Glove awards at third base, probably would have had franchises named after him if he'd played in a media-hot town, instead of Houston and San Diego. Rader has pulled a lot of stunts, such as switching the contents of the mouthwash and shave lotion bottles in the locker room, but he also has a deep side.

Here's another Rader: "I love the blankety-blank of a game. I love the camaraderie, the locker room jacking around. The bonding of men is what the anthropologists call it. No writer has really described that feeling of the locker room.

"They've written about it for men in war—Hemingway did it best—but not men in sports. Guys play out their stretch in baseball and they come back and visit the clubhouse for the camaraderie, the kidding around —that's what they're looking for because they don't find it anywhere else and they miss it. I know how I'd miss it."

Q: *Much has been written about the famed Chicago Cubs double-play combination, "Tinker-to-Evers-to-Chance." Who were the third baseman and manager of that team? —Izzy Goodman, Louisville.*

A: The forgotten man of baseball's most famous infield was Harry Steinfeldt. For the third straight year he had played 150 games at the hot corner in 1908, the year Franklin P. Adams penned the famous poem that began, "These are the saddest of possible words." Frank Chance, the first baseman, known as "The Peerless Leader," was the manager. Under Chance, the Cubs were in the World Series in four out of five years, won it twice.

Q: *Everyone knows that Ted Williams' career in*

major league baseball spanned four decades—the 1930s, 40s, 50s, and 60s. My question is: Did anyone play in the major leagues during the four decades of the 1940s into the 70s? If not, who came closest among those who started their careers in the late 1940s? I know Willie Mays started in 1951, but that's not the answer I'm looking for. I say Lew Burdette. —Robert Rolnick, Houston.

A: Funny you should ask. Through the courtesy of Bill Veeck, Orestes (Minnie) Minoso, at the age of fifty-three, returned to active duty in 1976 as a pinch hitter for the White Sox. Minoso broke in with Cleveland in 1949. Your man, Burdette, just missed, appearing as a rookie briefly with the Yankees in 1950, bowing out after the 1967 season. Others who came close were Mickey Mantle (1951–1968), Yogi Berra (1946–65), and Hank Aaron (1954–76).

Q: *How do famous athletes cope with the constant demands, the intrusions of people who pursue them in restaurants and at their hotels? I read once that Mickey Mantle had to take all his meals from room service during his best years with the Yankees because the fans wouldn't leave him alone in public. Is there any way they can protect their privacy without being rude? —Neal Praeger, Muncie.*

A: Home-run king Henry Aaron found a way. During the last three years of his baseball career, starting with the season he broke Babe Ruth's career record, Aaron led a dual identity. On the road his teams, the Atlanta Braves and then the Milwaukee Brewers, rented two rooms for him—one empty and registered in Aaron's name. The other room, listed under the name of Bill Suber, was where Henry slept. He was driven to that subterfuge by the midnight phone calls and knocks on his hotel door that kept him awake. The name was a variation of his second wife's maiden name, Billye Suber.

Q: *In this day of ridiculously high salaries for*

athletes, please tell me who was the first major league baseball player to receive $100,000 (just salary, not bonuses). I contend it was either DiMaggio, Williams, or Feller. Others say it was later—Mays or Mantle. Also, who were the first $100,000 players in the other sports? —Pat Feerick, c/o Terry's Tavern, Philadelphia.

A: In 1949, his eleventh season with the Yankees, Joe DiMaggio became baseball's first $100,000 man. The others to break the six-figure barrier were: John Unitas, football; Wilt Chamberlain, basketball; Bobby Orr, hockey.

The numbers game requires at least one footnote. Bill Russell of the Celtics made it a point of pride to be paid more than Chamberlain. When Wilt's record contract was announced by Philadelphia, Russell went to general manager Red Auerbach and demanded a raise. He was given a new contract for $100,001.

Q: *Can you please tell me some things about a Yankee ball player named George Stirnweiss? What position he played, his batting average, how long he played with them, and his age when he died. —James Stanlick, Rutherford, New Jersey.*

A: Although remembered by some as a "wartime" player, George Henry (Snuffy) Stirnweiss lasted ten years in the majors, the first seven with the Yankees. In 1945 he won the batting title with what was then the lowest average to qualify for that honor in forty years, .309. His lifetime mark was .268. He spent most of his career at second base, where in New York he succeeded the great Joe Gordon. Snuffy Stirnweiss died in 1958, a month before his fortieth birthday.

Q: *Do you know how the "Baltimore Chop" got its name when a player beats out an infield tap? — Israel Goodman, Louisville.*

A: Back in the 1890s when Wee Willie Keeler was hitting them where they ain't, and also running out a multitude of infield hits, the Baltimore infield was packed hard—to about the consistency of today's Astroturf. A perfect Baltimore Chop is a ball that bounces so high the runner gets to first before the infielder can get his hands on it.

Incidentally, Baltimore clay is the officially prescribed ingredient that umpires use to rub down the baseballs before every game.

Q: *Who was the oldest batting champion in the major leagues? That is, who won the batting title at the most advanced age? I say it has got to be Ty Cobb.* —*Red Quentin, Passaic, New Jersey.*

A: Cobb was a great hitter all his life (career average, .367), but the laurels on this one go to Teddy (Ballgame) Williams, who has hit .388 at age thirty-eight, and .328 at thirty-nine, both good for titles (1957–58). Williams is the only hitter who ever won a batting title past age thirty-five.

Q: *Are Mickey Mantle and Whitey Ford still close friends after all these years, or do they just put on an act for the beer commercial?* —*Jody Boatwright, Long Beach, California.*

A: The warmth you see is legitimate. Though Mantle's closest friend among ex-teammates is Billy Martin, he is still tight with Ford, Yogi Berra, and Elston Howard. Ford and Mantle also do a New York commercial for ice cream, and are teaming on a book by Joe Durso, *Mickey and Whitey,* which will be tapes of their reminiscences of the Yankee glory days.

Q: *Surely this must have been explained sometime in the past, but I want to know the origin of Yogi Berra's nickname.* —*T. H. Rappold, Detroit.*

A: Lawrence Peter Berra's playmates on the Hill in St. Louis thought the name "Yogi" denoted an oddball, spaced-out character. Old-time pal Joe Garagiola recalls one of their buddies who claimed Yogi was "always in a transom."

Q: *How much did Joe Garagiola get paid for doing all those TV programs with former President Ford, right before the election? Was it in line with what he usually gets for the baseball TV games?* —Andy Pressler, Chicago.

A: Garagiola donated his services to the President, so the question is not how much he got but how much it may have cost him. Some of the forty million people who voted for, and elected Jimmy Carter, might not approve the next time Garagiola appears on TV trying to sell them new automobiles.

Q: *When were the first summer Olympics held? Is there any record of the winners and the events?* —Chris Hamblen, Mount Vernon, New York.

A: The first Olympiad occurred in 776 B.C. and consisted of only one event, the 200-yard dash. The first to cross the finish line won the honor of taking a torch from a priest's hand and lighting the sacrificial pyre at an altar to Zeus. That first winner was a cook named Koroibos. His trophy was a laurel wreath from the sacred olive grove at Olympia. He was absolved from ever paying taxes and received free food and lodging for life.

Q: *Was football, not soccer but real football, ever a part of the Olympics? My grandfather maintains that it was.* —Jerry Weinstock, Yonkers, New York.

A: Not the U.S. brand of football. But rugby was an Olympic sport at Antwerp, Belgium, in 1920, and at Paris four years later. A team from the U.S., including fourteen players from California, won the 1924 Gold Medal by defeating France, 17–3, in the championship game. The French were so impressed that in addition to the Gold Medals they also presented each American with a specially designed Sevres vase.

185

Q *I know they didn't "streak," but didn't a couple of strippers create a sensation a few years ago running semi-nude through stadiums on the field? Who were they?* —Jan Glovan, Detroit.

A: The best known at the time, the late 60s, were Morgana Roberts, who specialized in baseball, and Bubbles Cash, the pro football fan. But they weren't semi-nude. In those dear bygone days, a miniskirt and snug T-shirt were enough to bring the house to attention. Morgana did her thing in several ball parks, once chasing Dodger Wes Parker from home plate to third base to plant a smooch on him. The opposing third baseman held Parker for her. Morgana also threatened to kiss President Nixon at the All-Star Game. The Secret Service stopped her. Had it happened, this might have changed the whole history of Watergate. The original streakers, by the way, were the Greek Olympians, who ran in the nude.